ENDANGERED PEOPLES

❖

What sets worlds in motion
is the interplay of differences, their attractions
and repulsions. Life is plurality, death is uniformity.
By suppressing differences and peculiarities,
by eliminating different civilizations and cultures,
progress weakens life and favors death, impoverishes and
mutilates us. Every view of the world that becomes
extinct, every culture that disappears,
diminishes a possibility of life.
Octavio Paz

❖

ENDANGERED PEOPLES

ART DAVIDSON

FOREWORD BY RIGOBERTA MENCHÚ, 1993 NOBEL PEACE PRIZE LAUREATE

PHOTOGRAPHS BY ART WOLFE AND JOHN ISAAC

BOOK DESIGN BY CHARLES FUHRMAN

SIERRA CLUB BOOKS ▲ SAN FRANCISCO

The Sierra Club, founded in 1892 by John Muir, has devoted itself to the study and protection of the earth's scenic and ecological resources—mountains, wetlands, woodlands, wild shores and rivers, deserts and plains. The publishing program of the Sierra Club offers books to the public as a nonprofit educational service in the hope that they may enlarge the public's understanding of the Club's basic concerns. The point of view expressed in each book, however, does not necessarily represent that of the Club. The Sierra Club has some sixty chapters coast to coast, in Canada, Hawaii, and Alaska. For information about how you may participate in its programs to preserve wilderness and the quality of life, please address inquiries to Sierra Club, 730 Polk Street, San Francisco, CA 94109.

Published by Sierra Club Books
100 Bush Street
San Francisco, CA 94104

First published in the United States, 1993

Text copyright © Art Davidson 1993
Photographs copyright © Art Wolfe and John Isaac 1993
Page 198 constitutes an extension of this copyright page.
Consulting editor: Daniel Moses, Director, Earth Island Press
Manuscript editor: Suzanne Lipsett
Typography: Steve Wozenski

10 9 8 7 6 5 4 3 2 1

ENDANGERED PEOPLES is produced by Brann & Company
Printed in Hong Kong

Library of Congress Cataloging-in-Publication Data
Davidson, Art 1943 –
ENDANGERED PEOPLES / text by Art Davidson;
with photographs by Art Wolfe and John Isaac
p. 208 cm.
ISBN: 0-87156-457-2 : $30.00

1. Indigenous peoples. 2. Environmental degradation. I. Title
GN380.D38 1993
306'.08—dc20

93-22026
CIP

*Previous page: Maasai mother
and daughter, Kenya.*

_____

*Opening double-page spread:
Indigenous children of the
Hunza Valley, Pakistan.*

C O N T E N T S

*F*reedom for indigenous peoples wherever they are—this is my cause. It was not born out of something good; it was born out of wretchedness and bitterness. It has been radicalized by the poverty of my people, the malnutrition that I as an Indian have seen and experienced, the exploitation I have felt in my own flesh, and the oppression that prevents us from performing our sacred ceremonies, showing no respect for the way we are.

At the threshold of the twenty-first century, the struggle of indigenous peoples to gain respect for their rights, identities, and aspirations is dynamic and increasingly widespread. It can no longer be denied or hidden by any of the groups seeking to perpetuate oppression and discrimination. The new millennium offers promise for those who have resisted for five hundred years in defense of their rights and their history.

We defend our roots not only to preserve them, but that they may flourish and bear fruit. In our struggle to gain respect for economic, social, cultural, civil, and political rights, we cannot agree to symbolic recognition or superficial concessions. Our aim is that all those rights should become effective at all levels: local, regional, and national. None of the grave and deep-rooted problems of the world can be resolved without the full participation of the indigenous peoples. Similarly, the indigenous peoples require the cooperation of the other sectors of society.

Many people have said that indigenous peoples are myths of the past, ruins that have died. But the indigenous community is not a vestige of the past, nor is it a myth. It is full of vitality and has a course and a future. It has much wisdom and richness to contribute. They have not killed us and they will not kill us now. We are stepping forth to say, "No, we are here. We live."

Rigoberta Menchú

Tibetan girl carrying firewood.

T oday, it is not distance but culture that separates the peoples of the world. How to cross such chasms between peoples may be the central question of our time.

"I am a dark-skinned, white-haired Indian grandmother, and sometimes I begin to feel that I am invisible," says Patricia Locke, a Lakota Indian and my close friend for nearly thirty years. "People see through me at airports, on the street, and at the meat market. When I mention this eerie feeling to Indian friends, they tell me it happens to them, too. I'm afraid to ask Indian children about it. I know this invisibility must hurt them. What is it that so clouds people's vision that they cannot see us?"

This sense of being invisible, unseen and misunderstood, so frustrating on a personal level, creates one of the cruelest ironies of our time. All around the world, enlightened people anxiously follow the fate of sea turtles, condors, spotted owls, black rhinos, and hundreds of other endangered species. But they forget—or never realize—that whole peoples can be endangered, too. Before our eyes, human diversity is vanishing, but few seem to notice. The battle lines of cultural survival cross every continent, but the skirmishes often take place out of the media's sight—hidden away in remote corners of a desert, a rain forest, an island, or a highland plain. In almost every country, indigenous peoples, the first people native to their lands, are fighting for their lives, their identities, and a future for their children.

There are still, by various counts, between two hundred and two hundred and fifty million indigenous people in the world. The threat to native peoples should not be mistaken for normal cultural evolution, which has always taken place. Over the course of human history, tribal people have emerged, migrated, joined with others, and faded away. But in our time as never before, distinct cultures are vanishing virtually overnight. Since the beginning of this century, more than ninety of Brazil's indigenous tribes have disappeared. The Chinese have forced countless Tibetans from their homeland and brutally suppressed those who remained. In

An Indian refugee from Guatemala, one of more than two hundred thousand who fled to Mexico.

• 1 •

Africa's Sudan, government troops have displaced three million tribal people. In Guatemala, in just the last fifteen years, forty-five thousand Indian women have become widows, two hundred thousand Indian children have been orphaned, and two million Indians have become refugees. In 1970, there were thirteen thousand Penan tribespeople living in the forests of Sarawak; two decades later there were fewer than five hundred. As this book goes to press, word arrives that the Penan are finished, gone.

This forced march into oblivion has many field marshals, all of them bolstered by our common indifference, misconceptions, misapprehensions, and distortions of the truth. By some people, native peoples are overly romanticized; by others, they are denigrated and seen as an obstacle to economic progress. But neither view is accurate. What indigenous peoples really share is a deep concern for the survival of their homes, their ways, their cultures . . . in a word, their individuality.

❖

Like many Americans, I saw my first Indian galloping across a television screen: It was Tonto riding his pinto alongside the Lone Ranger's white stallion. My first inkling that Indians were real people came to me when I was about nine. We lived in eastern Colorado, and after a wind storm in late March, I went out on the prairie with my father to look for arrowheads. I remember the first one I found. It was half buried in the sand, and as I bent over to pick it up, I suddenly realized that Indians, *Indians,* had actually *lived* here—right here among the rocks and sagebrush where I stood. Turning that carefully chipped piece of flint in my hand, I wondered for the first time, Where are they? Where did they go?

When I was twenty-one, I moved to Alaska, where I gradually began working with Native Alaskans, particularly Yup'ik and Cup'ik

Eskimos on the Bering Sea coast. In time, I was adopted by Joe Friday, a widely respected Cup'ik elder, and was taken into his extended Cup'ik family. Over the course of twenty-five years, I have witnessed and shared in many struggles— over land, over hunting and fishing rights, and over self-determination. Often I have heard native friends remark that they find themselves between two worlds—one foot in an ancient world, the other in the modern. I sometimes feel this way myself, but coming at the situation from the other direction. It is this dual perspective— with the native view illuminating my modern vantage point and vice versa—that I bring to this book.

In 1973, I worked closely with the Yup'ik chiefs—the Village Council Presidents, as they call themselves—to draft a statement on the state of their culture. The result was a small book titled *Does One Way of Life Have to Die So Another Can Live?* Since then, in my travels to many other parts of the world, I have found that native peoples everywhere are wrestling with this dilemma. Do their cultures have to die? Is it inevitable that the Indians of the Americas, the Aborigines, the Maoris, Igorots, Ainu, and hundreds of other distinct peoples will all be made to disappear?

The voices that speak in *Endangered Peoples* ring with the conviction that they are *not* going to disappear—not without a fight. All these groups know that the obstacles to their survival are tremendous, but the same is true of their determination. As Onondaga Chief Oren R. Lyons told the United Nations in 1992, "I stand before you as a manifestation of the spirit of our peoples and our will to survive. The catastrophes we have suffered at the hands of our brothers from across the sea have been unremitting and inexcusable. They crushed our peoples and nations. . . . Yet we survived."

But survival alone is not enough, and not what native peoples call for. Of all the obstacles indigenous peoples continue to face, one of the most fundamental is also the hardest for non-native people to grasp—that not everyone wants to join the mainstream. In the developed countries, many of us have grown so accustomed to our highways and shopping centers, careers and retirement plans, that we assume everyone everywhere desires our way of life, our material wealth, and all the conveniences and consequences that go with them. Yet native peoples all over the world echo the plea I first heard voiced by the Yup'ik elders of the village of Nightmute: "Please try to fathom our great desire to survive in a way somewhat different than yours."

In May 1992, this basic desire was given form and substance by more than four hundred indigenous leaders from the far corners of the earth. In Kari-Oca, Brazil, at the first World Conference of Indigenous Peoples, these delegates declared their desire "to walk to the future in the footprints of our ancestors . . . to maintain our inherent rights to self-determination, to decide our own form of government, to use our own laws, to raise and educate our children, to preserve our cultural identity."

This book is an attempt to cross the great distances between cultures. But as we begin to understand, *really understand,* the issues of indigenous peoples, we quickly confront the fact that the destinies of both native and nonnative peoples are linked. We all face challenges of survival. Among the greatest of these is the need for sustainable lifestyles that would enable us to live in balance with nature. It is a terrible irony that as our resource consumption reaches farther into rain forests and deserts, it destroys the only remaining cultures that know how to live in balance with the environment. Their cultural extinction would be a loss to us all.

To appreciate fully our global interdependence, we of the developed nations need to see the earth's native peoples for who they are, appreciating the problems they face and learning the value of their knowledge and wisdom. This book does not attempt to analyze the political and legal intricacies of their struggles to survive. But it bears witness to these realities and the urgency of returning to indigenous peoples their lands and their right to determine their own future.

For every culture described here, dozens of others might have been included. For every voice, every person's story, thousands of others are just as poignant and urgent. No matter where we live, our lives intertwine with those of indigenous peoples. No matter what the color of our skin or what language we speak, we all have a personal stake in their future. Our response to the survival crisis of indigenous peoples will determine whether our era will be remembered as the time when much human diversity disappeared—or that when the earth's peoples finally learned to live together.

Ishi, the last Yahi Indian, Northern California.

Previous page: In 1990, a Lakota rite of remembrance for Lakota killed at Wounded Knee one hundred years earlier.

*B*efore dawn on August 29, 1911, dogs began barking at the slaughterhouse just outside Oroville, California. The workmen who peered out into the gray light saw a half-naked man crouching against the corral fence. His hair was burned off close to his head. Strips of deer thong were strung through his earlobes, and a wooden plug was set in his nose. Dazed and bewildered, the last Yahi Indian had left his refuge in the mountains and stumbled into twentieth-century California.

The man, sturdy of build and in his forties, became a curiosity, a Stone Age relic. In time he learned to speak English, but he never spoke his given name aloud, as if the kernel of his identity had passed away when he entered the civilized world. The anthropologists who looked after him called him Ishi. His people had lived in Northern California for thousands of years before the arrival of settlers in the early 1800s; then they had numbered three to four thousand. At the time of first contact, they, like most Indians of North America, were hit hard by European diseases—such as measles, influenza, syphilis, and dysentery—to which they had no immunity, and 60 percent of the Yahi people died from these new illnesses. Disheartened but not yet broken, the survivors fought to protect their territory. The Yahi, who had no weapons of war, only their hunting bows and knives, were overwhelmed by the guns of the settlers.

"There are men in and around Chico who have sworn a great oath of vengeance that these Indians shall die a bloody death," wrote Stephen Powers in 1874. The Yahi, he reported, were "resisting civilization to the last man. . . . No human eye ever beholds them, except now and then some lonely hunter may catch a glimpse of a faint camp-fire, with figures flitting about it; but before he can creep within rifle-range the figures have disappeared."

The remnants of the Yahi nation sought refuge in remote canyons of the Sierra. When Ishi was nine years old, an incident known as the Kingsley Cave massacre pushed his people over the threshold toward extinction. In a remote mountain sanctuary, well stocked with food, more than thirty Yahi felt they were safe, but when four armed men led by Norman Kingsley found them, they had no escape. All but Ishi were killed on the spot. Later, Kingsley explained that during the shooting he switched from his Spencer rifle to a .38 caliber Smith & Wesson revolver because the rifle "tore them up so bad, particularly the babies."

The last remnant of the Yahi tribe gathered together and survived through concealment. During this time, Ishi grew to manhood. He and his small band moved camp often and always at night. It was a furtive existence, a desperate attempt to survive, and one by one over twenty years the others died. There came the day when Ishi had only one companion, and then he was alone. What unimaginable loneliness drew him down from the mountains to the outskirts of Oroville that August morning in 1911? His people had vanished, but not his will to live.

Ishi survived for four and a half more years, supported by the University of California in return for being a sort of living exhibit. After he died, his closest friend, Dr. S. T. Pope, said, "He looked upon us as sophisticated children—smart but not wise. We knew many things, and much that is false. He knew nature, which is always true. His were the qualities of character that last forever. He was kind; he had courage and self-restraint, and though all had been taken from him, there was no bitterness in his heart. His soul was that of a child, his mind that of a philosopher."

At about the time that the Yahi were enduring their prolonged struggle in the Sierra, another small band of California Indians disappeared virtually overnight—the result not of an armed attack, but of an attempt by missionaries to convert and assimilate them. In 1853, Roman Catholic padres at Mission Santa Barbara sailed to San Nicolas, a Channel Island seventy miles off the California coast. With promises of a better life, they convinced the San Nicolas islanders to return with them to the mission. After their boat put off from the island, it was discovered that a baby had been left behind. The captain refused to turn back, claiming that the landing would be too difficult. The baby's distraught mother jumped overboard and was last seen swimming toward the rocky shore. It was assumed that she died in the rough surf.

Within a few years, all of the San Nicolas Indians brought to the mission had died. Eighteen years later, seal hunters thought they spotted a lone woman on San Nicolas. A search party was sent out. They found the woman. Her child had died, and she was the sole survivor of her people. They brought her back to the mainland. Within a few months she too died, never having communicated with anyone.

The fate of this woman's people, and of Ishi and his, has been repeated many times in many ways. In addition, many nations of indigenous people, while not completely extinguished, have been reduced beyond recognition. Before the coming of Europeans, by various accounts between ten to thirty million people lived north of the Rio Grande—not merely tribes or bands or family groups of "Indians," a European term, but large, distinct nations, each with its own language, customs, rituals, territory, and complex belief system.

When the first Europeans arrived, more than four hundred Indian nations were prospering in what is now the United States. Some of these were brought down by armed ranchers, prospectors, and cavalry troops. Others lost their lands in the undeclared war of broken treaties— of more than four hundred treaties negotiated, few if any were fully honored. Diseases of European origin swept through every native nation, and although the epidemics may have never completely extinguished a culture, they often set peoples spiraling on a downward course.

Still other nations were coerced from their traditional ways of life by programs purporting or intending to help them.

By the early 1800s, many of North America's indigenous nations were losing their critical strength. William Clark, a leader of the 1804–1806 overland expedition to the Pacific, noticed that "before 1815 the tribes nearest our settlements were a formidable and terrible enemy; since then their power has been broken, their warlike spirit subdued, and themselves sunk into objects of pity and commiseration."

Even then it was widely held that Indians were on their way to complete extinction. "What can be more melancholy than their history? By a law of their nature, they seem destined to a slow, but sure extinction," wrote Justice Joseph Story, expressing the prevailing sentiment in 1828. "Everywhere, at the approach of the white man, they fade away. We hear the rustling of their footsteps, like that of withered leaves of autumn, and they are gone forever. They pass mournfully by us, and they return no more."

However, the Indians did not quite disappear. They took themselves farther out of sight, perhaps, but they were still around, and their presence became "inconvenient" to the westward expansion of the country. Increasingly, these fiercely independent peoples fell under the dictates of the U.S. government. The paternalistic relationship that developed took many forms, including "relocation," ostensibly for the Indians'

Navajo grandparents, Arizona. In the 1960s, the Navajo, the largest Native American tribe, still taught 90 percent of their children the Navajo language. In the thirty years since then, the U.S. Bureau of Indian Affairs has imposed English as a first language; as a result, most Navajo children speak only English.

benefit. Stubbornly refusing to vanish, the diverse native nations of North America became, collectively, the "Indian problem."

In 1835, President Jackson forced the Cherokees to give up all of their land east of the Mississippi in exchange for land in the Oklahoma Territory. "There your white brothers will not trouble you," he told them. "They will have no claim to the land, and you can live upon it, you and all your children, as long as the grass grows or the rivers run, in peace and plenty. It will be yours forever." Once the treaty was signed, the government ordered the Cherokees to walk to Oklahoma. Along the way, so many died that it became known as the Trail of Tears. By 1843, most of the eastern tribes had been either forcibly deprived of most of their land or coerced into moving west. In 1871, the General Allotment Act hammered another nail into the cultural coffin by breaking up many tribal governments and reservations, forcing Indians to assimilate into white society.

And always the numbers dwindled. In 1850, the U.S. Census counted only 400,764 Native Americans. Twenty years later, the official count was 313,712; by 1890 it stood at 248,253. Then something amazing and quite unexpected happened: the indigenous peoples of North America began to make a comeback. In 1938, John Collier, Commissioner of Indian Affairs, reported the "astounding and heartening fact" that the Indians were increasing in numbers faster than any other segment of the American population. Said Collier, "For nearly three hundred years white Americans, in our zeal to carve out a nation made to order, have dealt with the Indians on the erroneous, yet tragic assumption that . . . [they] were a dying race."

In response, Congress passed the Indian Reorganization Act of 1934 "to rehabilitate the Indian's economic life and give him a chance to develop the initiative destroyed by a century of oppression and paternalism." But in 1953,

perhaps to temper the success of this policy, Congress abruptly changed course, ending federal support services and forcing the dissolution of many reservations. This new policy was called *termination,* and over the next ten years one hundred and nine Indian nations were forced to dissolve their tribal governments.

While the number of Indian people continued to increase, termination helped perpetuate the perception of Indians as a lost and dying race, usually to their detriment. If the Indians are dying out, then they might, at least subliminally, be dismissed as fascinating but politically inconsequential, romanticized and mourned but not be a population to take seriously. After all, Ishi lived out his life on display at a museum, a living exhibit that people paid to see. And there is still a tendency for Americans to be more comfortable with native peoples as tourist attractions or some mythical idealization than as real people.

I recall that day when I was nine years old, holding a piece of chipped flint in my hand and wondering, Where have they gone? I now know that we have already pushed some of our continent's peoples to extinction. These groups came down to one individual, like Ishi or the San Nicolas woman, and then vanished forever. Others have been here all along. Of these remaining groups, some are doing well, but many are still struggling to survive.

The 1990 U.S. Census counted one million nine hundred thousand Native Americans, one-fourth of whom were Cherokees and Navajos. Most of the five hundred and forty-two other tribes listed had fewer than a thousand members. And some tribes had only a handful of members, the last living repositories of their people's customs and ties to the land.

❖

How does a culture come undone? Sometimes a single tragedy is the decisive turning point: people lose their lands or their hunting and fishing rights, or a dam floods a community. But more often than not, a host of factors, some obvious and others quite subtle, press and pull a nation one way and another, until it, and the individuals that make it up, becomes something quite different from what it was. The unraveling of a culture can start one thread at a time, as one person after another stops speaking the native language and loses the traditional ways of singing and praying.

Without its language, a people might survive physically but not culturally. "I'm sure that a hundred years from now, there will be dark-skinned people with black hair running around this region," says Yup'ik Eskimo leader Harold Napoleon. "But will they be Yup'ik? Will they speak Yup'ik? Will they think Yup'ik? Will they have our values? Will they be free?"

Marie Smith, the last Eyak Indian, Cordova, Alaska.

"People who lose their language lose part of themselves," Pete Catches, a Lakota medicine man, once told me. For not just words are lost when a language goes; so are the stories, songs, and ceremonies that once gave young people a shared sense of who they were. Perhaps the white legislators knew this when, in 1886, they prohibited the use of any Indian language: "No books in any Indian language must be used or instruction given in that language. . . . The rule will be strictly enforced." Three years later, a supplemental report asserted that "education should seek the disintegration of the tribes."

This was the policy of assimilation, of forcing Indians to talk and think like whites. This policy has now been disavowed, but its effects live on. Of the six hundred native languages that once flourished in North America, only a hundred and fifty-five are still spoken. Of these, forty-five are on the brink of extinction. Only thirty-eight are still being learned by the children.

❖

"I am the only one left now. The only full-blooded Eyak. The only one who speaks the language," says Marie Smith. "I don't know why it's me, why I'm the one. I tell you, it hurts. It really hurts."

She lives near my home outside Anchorage, Alaska, and sometimes we sit at her kitchen table, sipping cups of strong coffee. At seventy-four, she is white-haired and wrinkled but still hearty. Marie lights a cigarette. I am about to compliment her on her home, when she says, "It hurts me to live here in the city. I love being at sea. I have to be near the water. You know, I went on a boat when I was four days old.

"My father was the last Eyak chief, and I've taken his place. I'm the chief now, and I have to go down to Cordova to try to stop the clear-cutting on our land. It's no good. You may think this strange. Maybe you'll laugh, but we always prayed to what we took. Before cutting down a tree, we'd say, 'Forgive us, understand that we need your warmth.' That's what my father taught me."

Marie reminisces about her people and the land where they flourished. She grew up where the Copper River winds out of the Wrangell Mountains to form a vast delta at the edge of Prince William Sound. Each spring, now as then, tens of thousands of ducks and geese come to nest on the grassy gravel bars, and millions of shorebirds stop to feed on their way north. Grizzlies, wolves, coyotes, and foxes hunt birds and small mammals along the edge of the tidal flats. During the summer months, spawning salmon fight their way up the river channels.

Eyak villages once dotted the edges of the sound and appeared as far as two hundred miles south at Cape Yakataga. The exact circumstances of their evolution remain a mystery, but the Eyak evidently split off from other Athabascan tribes. They lived at the edge of the sea, but they were not a sea-faring people like the Tlingits to the south and the Chugach Eskimos to the west. The less aggressive Eyak were a gentle people who caught salmon in the rivers, gathered clams and mussels, and hunted birds and mountain goats. Generation after generation came and went like the winter snows and summer salmon—until a fateful twist of circumstances about a hundred years ago began to take the Eyak culture apart. Though they didn't know it growing up, Marie Smith and her cousin, Anna Nelson Harry, were to be in the last generation of their people.

When Marie was a little girl, there were five Eyak families in her village. Among them were the parents of Anna, who was born in 1906, the year Cordova was founded four miles from Eyak Lake. While Anna was still an infant, her father died. Her earliest memories were of the raw side of newly developing frontier life. Canneries sprang up, blocking the best Eyak fishing streams; salmon were dynamited to the surface.

The men who came to the canneries for work brought alcohol, opium, measles, tuberculosis, and syphilis to the Eyak. There were few women around, so the competition for them was fierce and often violent. At age six, Anna watched helplessly as a man brutally murdered her pregnant mother. Orphaned, she turned to other nearby villages for food and shelter. To stay warm in winter, she often had to curl up with the dogs to sleep near an open fire. Infections festered on her neck. She believed the dogs licking her open wounds finally healed the sores. The scars never disappeared.

At age twelve, Anna married Galushia Nelson, an Eyak from neighboring Alaganik. They were making a new start for themselves and for the Eyak, but shortly after their marriage, Anna was abducted and raped by cannery workers. It took Galushia several weeks to find her and get her back. Together they had four sons. He supported their family as a mechanic, but shortly after the birth of their last child, he died of tuberculosis. Anna raised their children the best she could. Cash was always scarce, but they gathered food from the land.

Anna turned to storytelling, focusing with a lively humor on the relationships between humans and animals. One of her favorite stories tells of a young woman abducted by a pack of wolves. In their home in the mountains, the wolves were kind to her, sharing all their food with her. One day she left the wolves and returned to her people. "Don't keep killing the wolves that way any more," she told them. "They are just people like us," she said. "All these things have spirits—the wolves, black bears, mountain goats, all these living beings. The wolf people told me about this. Their spirits speak to us."

As Cordova grew, the Eyak dwindled away. Eventually, Anna left her ancestral home near Cordova for Yakutat, on the coast. She outlived all her children and her other relatives. Shortly before she died in 1975, Anna said, "I walk around the beach at low tide. I sit down on a rock. I just break into tears. My uncles all died out on me. After my uncles all died out, my aunts fell to die. . . . The Eyaks, they are all dying off. . . . Like the ravens, I'll live alone."

Sitting quietly at her kitchen table, Marie pours me another cup of coffee. Now that Anna has passed away, Marie is the last of her people. She has twenty-eight grandchildren, but they are of mixed blood and have lost the language and ways of the Eyak people. Even they regard Marie as the last Eyak.

We sit in silence for a few moments.

Then she says, "These days, I hear my father talking to me. He tells me to go ahead and do what I have to do."

"What do you feel you have to do?" I ask. She is quiet for a moment, looks out the window, and then turns toward me.

"I want our people to let go of their hate. We've been pushed around so much. Battered this way and that. But it's not our way to feel hatred in our hearts. Or the greed that even some of our own people have today. That's not the Indian way to be. My dream is to let the greed and hate go and bring back the old ways."

Vincent Tumamait was one of the last handful of traditional singers and storytellers of the Chumash people, who once thrived along the two-hundred-mile stretch of the California coast between Malibu and San Luis Obispo. Vincent believed that even though a people's numbers may be few, its customs, values, and wisdom can be revived and shared with others. A few months before he passed away in 1992, Vincent gave the opening address at a memorial for Ishi; he sang a healing song of his ancestors and spoke of the special meaning that Ishi's life holds for us all.

YUP'IK

THE WAY OF THE HUMAN BEING

So you're one of those conservationists," said the young Eskimo man with a hint of challenge in his voice. "You like the wild geese and seals and want to protect them?"

"Yeah, I like wildlife," I said. I'd just met this guy and already he was testing me. "I like waterfowl and seals, and sometimes they do need protection."

"Well, I like seals, too. I like to hunt them," he said. "We'd starve without them. What do you think about that?"

"There are just so many seals in the ocean," I said. "If we all hunted them, they'd be gone pretty soon, wouldn't they? So I'll stick to beef, and you guys can go after the seals."

He looked at me and smiled—and so began one of the great friendships of my life. We began working together, and over the past twenty years this Yup'ik Eskimo, Harold Napoleon, and I have shared many battles to protect both animals and people. In the process, we have come to regard each other as brothers.

Yet we come from strikingly different backgrounds. I am of Scottish and Irish descent and grew up in an old Victorian house in eastern Colorado. My father was an artist. Harold comes from a long line of *angalkuq*, or shamans. His father provided for his family by hunting and fishing, and Harold was born when his family was returning by boat from a berry-picking camp. With a late summer storm blowing in from the Bering Sea, there was no time to pitch a tent, so they tipped their boat on its side for a windbreak. His Aunt Aldine cut the umbilical cord with an *ulu* knife, and, as Harold tells it, "I was born right onto the grass into a world that no longer exists."

There were always two worlds for Harold—the ancient and the modern— and they seemed to be forever realigning and rebalancing their presence within him. "Sometimes I think I was never young," he once told me. "My friends were old men. I wanted to hear their stories. I wanted to know how it used to be. Even when I was very young, I thought like an old man."

At the age of five, Harold made a discovery that would have a profound effect on his life —reading. And it was Latin that he learned first. As an altar boy, he pestered Jesuit Father Donahue into teaching him how to read the Latin liturgy. With Yup'ik spoken at home and Latin in church, English became Harold's third language when he started school; there he started reading everything he could get his hands on. But while books opened up the world of ideas and distant places, life at home had its own harsh realities. Sometimes his family would have only one meal a day.

"We were really poor in those days. We were going hungry," he recalls. "It was the poverty we lived in and the discrimination I knew as a child that made me want to change things when I grew up. By the age of eight or nine, I was already preoccupied with my people. I knew I was going to serve them."

Harold was to become a leader of a generation maturing in a cultural no-man's-land. The young people were caught in the crossfire of conflicting values, languages, and ways of being. The old Yup'ik world was disintegrating and the new world was, at best, confusing. Eskimo people traditionally look to elders for guidance, but in this uniquely difficult time they turned to Harold Napoleon. In August 1972, when he was barely twenty-two, the elders asked him to be director of their Association of Village Council Presidents, the most important position of leadership in his region.

I began working with Harold as a natural resource advisor. One of the first trips we took together was to Mekoryak. There we met with nearly all the villagers who gathered in the quonset hut that served as a community center. The lights periodically flared and dimmed as the village generator surged and faded. Women sat on the floor, many with restless babies in their laps. Most of the men stood along the wall with their arms folded. No sooner had Harold begun

describing the recently enacted Alaska Native Claims Settlement Act than an old man in the back of the room asked, "What is this land claims act you are talking about? Where does it come from? Who decided these things?"

In the rush to pass the land claims act, Congress had imposed Western concepts and institutions on village people—people who had their own tribal ways of relating to the land—without even consulting with them. The very concept of land ownership was foreign to the Yup'ik. They considered land to be simply part of the world we live in, like the sky or ocean. I remember ninety-year-old Alena Nikolas saying, "When I was growing up, there weren't any of these little lines and areas drawn on a map— regulations or boundaries. Nobody would come around and say, 'This is my land, that is your land.' These lands were everybody's. People lived happily together. We were happy then."

"Congress decided our future without taking the time to talk with us," said Harold. "I always felt like we were being ruled. State and federal agencies ran everything. We had no control over our lives. I wanted us to run our own lives. And I believed strongly that we had rights. I wanted us to be free."

But there was no end to how others wanted to control Yup'ik lands and the Yup'ik way of life. Oil companies were eager to explore for oil. Entrepreneurs came up with money-making schemes. Conservationists proposed more regulations without checking with the native people. Others were forever telling Yup'iks what to do—and how to do it. Harold took on every challenge—helping villages protect their land, health services, housing. And he was continually fending off threats to his people's way of life, which was based on hunting and fishing. To empower the Yup'ik people with their own grass roots conservation organization, he formed Nunam Kitlusti, Protectors of the Land.

Above all, Harold fought for Yup'ik

children. The school system was leaving them torn between the traditional and modern worlds, and unprepared to live in either. While native teaching always encouraged children to share and serve their families and community, Western education was telling them to compete, promote themselves, beat the other guy. "When our children come back educated, they are no longer the same children we saw leave for school," a mother once told us. "Some of our children become strangers to their own people. But much worse, they are strangers to themselves."

To help the young people find themselves, Harold developed a cultural heritage program that brought teenagers and elders together. For two weeks, the students would put aside geom-

etry and American history to learn the arts and skills of their people. In one village on the lower Kuskokwim River, I watched two men in their sixties patiently show high school basketball players how to make snowshoes: bending the wood, cutting strips of leather, stringing the webbing. Another group of boys carefully cut and wove thin strips of willow into a fish trap. It is hard to describe how the faces of these young people lit up when they caught their first fish in a trap that had been part of a willow tree the day before.

It was Harold's conviction that the Yup'ik way of life could be saved and that only the young could save it. He was close to his son Olin, and in time his family grew with the births of Alison, a quiet and sensitive girl, and the youngest, George,

Harley Sundown, fishing for herring in the Bering Sea off the northwest coast of Alaska.

Harold Napoleon. Paimute, Alaska. "The survivors who escaped the Great Death staggered dazed and confused into the new world. Locked inside their souls were memories of the spirit world, of the way life used to be, and of the horrors they had witnessed."

a very bright and cheerful child. "This little George asks questions about everything," Harold would say. "He follows me everywhere. So I'm going to teach him everything I know. He'll know our language, how to live off the land, all the old ways. He will know he is a real Eskimo, and he's going to help our people some day. And do you know what this little George tells me? He says, 'Daddy, I love you here to the mountains. Here to the mountains, Dad.'"

But as the years passed, Harold's frustrations and despair mounted as his people were hit with one crisis after another—loss of hunting and fishing rights, imposition of new laws, erosion of the rural economy, and the never-ending clash over values with the dominant culture. No matter how hard Harold worked and how much progress he made, the pain, confusion, and alienation of his people increased. Fetal alcohol syndrome, which results from excessive maternal drinking during pregnancy, became prevalent

among native women. Suicide became epidemic. Teenagers took their own lives with knives, guns, and grain alcohol. Alakanuk, a village of five hundred and fifty, typified the vicious cycle of self-destruction. In sixteen months, there were eight suicides, dozens of other attempts, two murders, and four drownings. The suicide rate for Alaska native men grew to ten times that for other American men.

Many nights, I saw Harold agonize over the despair of the Yup'ik young people. Grade school children used cigarettes to burn holes in their skin. Some died sniffing glue. One day a teenager might be playing basketball or dancing with friends; the next day he or she was gone. There might be a note left behind about life not making any sense, but usually there was nothing. One mother saw her daughter grab a shotgun and blow away the upper part of her body. A father came upon his sixteen-year-old son with his wrists slashed, lying in a pool of blood. A young woman was found in a snowstorm, lying naked and frozen beside the road. Surrounded by such suffering, even the most capable and confident leader must feel that he is failing his people.

"Their problems became mine," Harold said. "Naively, I thought I could solve them all, but needless to say, I did not. Perhaps I took myself and my responsibility too seriously, but it was what I perceived to be my failures and the subsequent frustration and anger that led to my becoming an alcoholic."

As Harold's drinking increased, his moods swung sharply, sometimes into depression. One evening in the spring of 1984, he appeared at my house overwhelmed with despair. "I'm going to die," he said. "I have lived for my people. I've done everything I can. It feels hopeless. There is no more I can do. . . . My life is over."

Three weeks later, I got a call to come to the Cook Inlet Pretrial Facility. Coils of razor wire looped over the concrete walls. Bars encased every exterior window. Inside, steel doors clanged

Margaret Temple, Napakiak, Alaska.

and guards' voices echoed sharply as I was led to a small room. On the other side of a thick, bullet-proof glass partition sat Harold, gaunt, his skin ashen. His black hair was disheveled and his eyes were red and nearly swollen shut from days of crying. His face quivered every time he tried to say the name of his four-year-old son, George, whom he was accused of killing.

"I live a minute at a time," he said. "Fifteen minutes is an eternity. I didn't know there was such pain."

"What happened?" I asked.

"I don't know," he said. "I can't remember anything."

Investigators concluded that Harold's son George had been struck with a blunt object. We were stunned. Like others who knew Harold well, I found it impossible to believe that he had harmed his son. Harold was the hope of his generation, the most capable leader at the most crucial time in the history of his people. Everyone knew how much he loved his children, and the last person to see Harold and his son together said that he was playing with his boy lovingly. There were no witnesses to his son's death. But Harold had been drinking. He was charged with second-degree murder.

"I've lost both my son and my man," said his wife, Francine, who had been in another village when their son died. "But I don't hate

Harold. I don't even feel like I have to forgive him, because I don't believe he is guilty. Harold never, ever hit our children. He never abused them."

Harold's testimony and the statements of those who knew him best were never given to a jury. Harold himself had been wounded the night his son died, but photographs indicating that he may have been protecting himself and his son from an intruder were never presented as evidence. When his day in court arrived, Harold refused to defend himself.

"I'm hurting so much that I could not survive a trial. I would die," he told me. "No father ever wants to live through something like this. This was my son. I loved him. I cannot imagine hurting him. And I will not accept the accusation that I hurt him on purpose. But somehow, because I was drinking, I caused my son's death. I was unable to protect him when he needed to be protected. It was my fault. I am responsible."

Harold pleaded no contest to second-degree murder. At sentencing, he told the judge, "I want to be a reminder of what alcohol can do. Then maybe my son's death won't be in vain." The court found that Harold had never previously harmed any child, and then sentenced him to twenty-five years in prison. This man, who had once struggled so fiercely for the rights of his people, now fought his hardest battle from the loneliness of his cell. His sentence, harsh as it was, meant nothing compared to his profound grief.

Yup'ik boy with his dogs on the Yukon-Kuskokwim Delta.

As the hours of agony stretched into years, Harold had time to ponder the broken pieces of his life and the lives of his people.

"I've learned things in prison that I could never have learned anywhere else," Harold told me during one of my visits. "Things I once took for granted I now value: just walking on the tundra and feeling its richness, going out on the Bering Sea, watching animals. And I've learned that the way native people are living is killing them. Filling the prisons. Maiming. Crippling the children. It is unacceptable. But we have been so brutalized that we are accepting the abnormal. People die of loneliness and heartbreak and sorrow. They just give up."

At times, Harold felt like giving up himself. Instead, he took a terrifying but ultimately healing journey into his grief. From the well of confusion and hurt, Harold looked through the ruins of his life to the troubles his parents had faced and to the suffering of their parents. Gradually, he began to see that his people had changed fundamentally with the arrival of white people—and with the diseases they had brought.

I visited Harold whenever I could. One day, as I was preparing to leave, he asked me to wait for a moment. He went back to his cell and returned with a blue spiral notebook. "Here, Art, I want you to read this," he said. "One night, it all fell into place. I wrote for eighteen hours. I couldn't stop. It all came out."

He called it *Yuuyaraq, The Way of the Human Being.* Copies were soon being handed from friend to friend, and within a year the University of Alaska had published it. It begins this way: "For the last seven years I have been in prison as a direct result of my alcoholism. I have spent this time grieving, not only for my son, but for the others who have died in this long night of our suffering. There is no greater sorrow than for a man to lose his son and know that he is responsible. I've descended into the darkest corner of our native world. And it's frightening there. I have been in that very dark place where all hope is gone. There is no life there. I know where the kids are when they kill themselves. I've been there. I now see why so many lives are lost to suicide, homicide, and accidents."

By staring into the disintegration of the Yup'ik people, Harold saw more deeply than he ever had before into the grief of his people and the ethnic divisions increasingly plaguing the globe. Wherever Europeans had arrived in the western hemisphere, indigenous peoples had experienced a common trauma: battles over values and beliefs followed by diseases such as measles and smallpox. For the Yup'ik, the "Great Death" began with influenza. Wherever a vast sweep of death wiped away thousands, even millions, virtually overnight, the trauma did not pass away with the victims but lived on in the survivors, crippling them and their children.

"We all carry the trauma of that Great Death," he wrote. "Our children inherit the trauma—the unresolved pain and grief is being passed from generation to generation. *This* is the source of our desperation, not simply the insult to our traditional ways, but this deep well of loss. To dampen the pain we anesthetize ourselves with alcohol. We have to end this vicious cycle of evil in our lives. We have to sober up. And we have to heal the wounds that lie behind our alcoholic abuse. Many native people suffer from an illness that infects their spirit. It's as if we had lost our soul."

Harold saw that the cure for alcoholism, an illness of the spirit, must be of the spirit as well. And for matters of spirit he looked to the old Yup'ik world in which his people had lived free and secure. In the Yup'ik way of life, which was very old and complete, *Yuuyaraq* was "the way of being a human being." Although unwritten, it governed all aspects of a human being's life, defining correct behavior between people and among all living things. In those times, all things had spirit and every occurrence had a spiritual cause. The medicine man—the *angalkuq*—understood the spirit world and was the interpreter of *Yuuyaraq*. He is said to have gone to the moon, to the bottom of the sea, and to the bowels of the earth in his search for understanding and solutions for his people's problems.

All this began to change when the first white men arrived on the Bering Sea coast. At first, the Yup'iks fought off the Russian traders who tried to colonize them and resisted the Christian priests who urged them to abandon their spirit world. However, their will was soon sapped; traders, whalers, and missionaries brought in diseases for which the Yup'ik had no immunity. In 1900, an influenza epidemic originated in Nome and spread like wildfire to all corners of Alaska. Not knowing about bacteria or viruses, the old Yup'ik attributed illnesses to a defect in their spirit.

"The confusion, suffering, and despair were unimaginable," Harold wrote of the Great Death. "Children watched helplessly as their mothers, fathers, brothers and sisters grew ill. First one family would begin to vomit and shake with fever—then another, and another. The efforts of the *angalkuq* failed. Families died. Entire villages disappeared. Here and there, a child or an adult would be spared. Even the exhausted medicine men grew ill and died in despair. And with them died a great part of *Yuuyaraq*, the ancient spirit world of the Eskimo. The survivors woke up bewildered and afraid. Like soldiers on a battlefield strewn with the dead, they were shell-shocked. They grieved and felt guilty for having survived." Harold came to realize that the Yup'ik survivors of the Great Death were suffering from post-traumatic stress syndrome.

The men and women orphaned by the sudden and traumatic death of their culture became the first generation of the modern-day Yup'ik. In their weakened and confused condition, they repressed their pain and buried their old culture in the silence of denial. Yup'ik parents stopped teaching their children and gave them over to the missionaries and schoolteachers, who washed their mouths with soap if they spoke their native language. Disoriented and weakened, the survivors allowed newcomers to take over their lives. Traditional dances and feasts disappeared. Drums were thrown away or hidden. The parents allowed these things to happen because they were ashamed of who they were, and they passed this shame on to their children.

"For survivors of the Great Death, escape becomes a necessity," wrote Harold. "They drink and take drugs. Suppressing the traumatic experience drives it into their psyche, or soul, where it festers and begins to control their lives. Their children inherit their despair, loneliness, confusion, and guilt. Not knowing why they feel this way, they begin looking down on their own people, seeing them as quaint, ignorant, and laughable. Several generations of suppressed anger, confusion, and feelings of inferiority and powerlessness now permeate even the very young. They are ashamed to be Yup'ik and try to become like white people. They give up everything—their culture, their language, their spiritual beliefs, their songs, their dances, their feasts, their lands, their independence, their identity. They disappear into themselves, wrapping their unbearable emotions in a deep silence.

"We have been wandering in a daze for a hundred years. Denial and silent suffering have become traits of our people. Is this to be our way of life till the end, burying the victims of the victims? Or can we resurrect a healthy way of life—a new *Yuuyaraq* for the present world?"

The wounds of a hundred years of suffering do not heal overnight. Alaska natives need time to heal and the chance to do it on their own, reasserting the independence and self-reliance that were once the marks of the Yup'ik people. As Harold put it, "Native people must regain their souls. We must take risks and deal directly with life's hardships, in order to regain our identity and spirituality. We must release the trauma. Then mothers will begin to see their sons for the first time, sons will see their fathers for the first time. Then, we can all go home again, become families and villages. Otherwise, we will cease to exist as a people. It is a matter of survival.

"The way we are living now is abnormal, the life of a caged animal," he wrote. "From birth to death, Alaska natives are cared for by the government. We are fed, housed, watered, cared for, but we are not free. To continue to assimilate native people, trying to remake them into anything else but what they are, is to slowly kill them. The only way to end our suffering is for villages and tribes to reassert their responsibilities for governing, clothing, and housing their people. We have to reestablish a sense of 'sovereignty.'"

On February 23, 1993, Harold Napoleon was paroled after serving eight years of his sentence. He began working at the Alaska Native Foundation to secure the rights of governance and self-determination that would free Alaska's native people. In response to his paper, *Yuuyaraq,* several churches apologized for how the actions of their missionaries had contributed to the trauma of the Great Death. With both native and nonnative leaders seeking his counsel, Harold developed an entirely new approach to the problems of Native Alaskans. Self-reliance and self-healing are the keystones in a move away from dependence on the government, as whole villages look within to confront and overcome the wounds left by the Great Death.

Mary and the late Joe Friday of Chevak. "In those old times," Joe once said, "everything the land provided was used for daily living. The parents and elders taught the children the knowledge they needed to survive in this harsh land. Life was not easy then. Life is easier now, but not as satisfying."

GWICH'IN

PEOPLE OF THE CARIBOU

*T*he Brooks Range, a nine-hundred-mile sweep of jagged peaks and winding rivers, arcs across northern Alaska and into Canada. Near the Canadian border, the glacier-fed waters of the Chandalar River flow south from the range. Where the river leaves the mountains and meanders out from the foothills, a cluster of small log houses, a school, a church, and a community center stand above the bank. This is Arctic Village, one of fifteen villages in Alaska and northwestern Canada that are home to the Gwich'in, the northernmost Indians of North America.

Several miles east of the village is a clearing where caribou often come out of the trees to eat, drink, and rest. The grass is thick here, the omnipresent mosquitoes less pesky than elsewhere, and in their need to remain alert for wolves and bears, the caribou can see for some distance as they graze. Lincoln Tritt of Arctic Village recalls: "As long as I can remember, every spring and fall, someone would always be sitting by a campfire on the hilltop, keeping a lookout for caribou. The hill is visible from the village, so if this person saw caribou, he would wave or make his fire give off more smoke. Then the village would come to life, and people would run up there. We all seemed to be at our best at these gatherings. We were filled with happiness and sharing. This was an especially important time for me as a child. It meant that for those brief, bright moments my friends and I were 'men.'"

Lincoln grew up in Arctic Village, went away to college, and then returned home. He recounted the changes he perceived. "Gradually, our human and spiritual values are being replaced by monetary values, which our people are still trying to make sense of. Traditionally, the value of money and the concept of 'me' are foreign to our people. We have always done things as a group and thought in terms of the tribe and the family. I wish the world would stop a minute and, like the man on the hill watching for caribou, see what is really happening."

As the Plains Indians once depended upon buffalo, the Gwich'in depend upon caribou. They speak of their relationship to the caribou as a kind of kinship.

A Gwich'in child, Arctic Village, Alaska.

It began long ago, they say, in a time when all creatures spoke the same language. In that distant time, the caribou and the Gwich'in people were one. As they evolved into separate beings, every caribou kept a bit of the human heart and every human retained a bit of caribou heart. In this way, the caribou and Gwich'in would always be able to sense each other's thoughts and feelings. The tundra would sustain the caribou and the caribou would sustain the people.

Ancient memories and history flow together. Ancestors of the Gwich'in evolved their intimate relationship with the caribou long before the first stirrings of Western civilization. Peering back into prehistory, archaeologists have found evidence that caribou have roamed this region for at least fifty-four thousand years. Bone artifacts from the Old Crow River in Canada indicate the presence of humans twenty-seven thousand years ago.

Today about five thousand Gwich'in live in Alaska and Canada, and until recently most of them were content to live quietly in their corner of the world, letting the commotion of the twentieth century pass them by. It was fine if their way of life went unnoticed and unknown. By the 1980s, however, their cherished isolation had come to an end: Oil companies were moving to drill in the calving grounds of the Porcupine caribou herd. Fearing that the caribou would go the way of the buffalo, the Gwich'in concluded that they had to fight back.

"Before we were threatened by oil development in the caribou calving grounds, we tried to keep to ourselves. But now we have to talk to others," says Sarah James of Arctic Village. Although neither chief nor elder, Sarah has emerged as a leader in this current crisis. "Maybe there are too few of us to matter. Maybe people think Indians are not important enough to consider in making their energy decisions. But it's my people who are threatened by this development. We are the ones who have everything to lose."

Across the border in Canada, another Gwich'in woman, Norma Kassi of Old Crow, expressed the same gnawing anxiety. "A long shadow now hangs over our lives," she said. "Oil development threatens the caribou. If the caribou are threatened, then the people are threatened. Oil executives and American senators don't seem to understand. They don't come into our homes and share our food. They have never tried to understand the feelings expressed in our songs and our prayers. They have never seen the faces of our elders light up when they hear that the caribou have come back. And they have not seen our elders weep when they think about the damage that oil rigs would cause to the caribou. Our elders have seen parts of our culture destroyed and are worried that our people may disappear forever."

❖

The Gwich'ins' current struggle to protect their way of life began in 1968, with the discovery of oil in Prudhoe Bay. The oil companies' permit to build the Trans-Alaska Pipeline hinged on the settlement of Alaska natives' long-pending land claims by Congress. While most Native Alaskans agreed to accept title to some lands and cash payment for others, the Gwich'in opted to forgo any cash benefit in favor of retaining control over a larger area of land. Their objective was to protect the caribou—and thus their way of life. But the sense of security they gained through this agreement was short-lived. By the mid-1980s, oil companies and the State of Alaska began lobbying to drill for oil in the calving grounds of the Porcupine caribou herd, which lay within the Arctic National Wildlife Refuge.

To understand the threat to the Porcupine herd, one needs to appreciate the ecological role of these remarkable creatures. The herd takes its name from the Porcupine River, which originates in Canada's far north, crosses the border into Alaska, and flows into the Yukon, forming the major watershed of the herd's range. Each spring, a hundred and sixty thousand caribou make an incredible sixteen-hundred-mile migration. Heading north from their wintering grounds in the Boreal Forest of Canada's Yukon Territory, they cross the Alaska border, swim the turbulent Porcupine River, and pour through passes in the Brooks Range. Descending from the mountains, they fan out across the Arctic coastal plain, where they give birth to their calves.

Once, while mountain climbing, I came upon the herd high in the Brooks Range. The land was still; there was not a breath of wind. Then the horizon seemed to move. The far hills were shimmering, as if reflecting heat waves. It was the caribou. Like a wave of mist over the tundra, thousands of cows with calves were coming up the valley. Soon they were so close I could hear the clicking of their hooves. Occasionally,

youngsters would sprint off madly, dash up a hill, turn and wheel in tight circles, and bound after each other. Just days before, these calves had bonded with their mothers by scent and sound. Now they were taking chances, playing with reckless energy, developing the stamina and quick agility that would help them outrun bears or wolves.

Over thousands of years of trial and error, the caribou have chosen the flat expanse at the edge of the Arctic Ocean as the best place for their calves to survive, since it provides an abundance of nutritious grass and some relief from predators. By mid-May, the first bands of pregnant cows reach the Arctic National Wildlife Refuge, instinctively timing their arrival to coincide with the sprouting of new grass shoots. The first calves are born by the end of May. After

In the Gwich'in story of their people's beginnings, they and the caribou evolved together.
Their lives remain entwined to this day.

Sarah James of Arctic Village. "We take care of the land and it takes care of us. If we destroy it, what are we doing to our children? Without the land we are nobody."

feeding on the lush grasses and lichens through June and early July, the herd begins moving south, back through the mountains toward their winter range in Canada. Along the way, the caribou help sustain wolves, grizzlies, and the Gwich'in.

Before the coming of European trappers, Gwich'in hunted caribou with arrows and spears, sometimes corraling them with carefully positioned spruce-pole fences. Today Gwich'in hunters use rifles and snowmobiles, but their traditional approach to the hunt remains unchanged. No matter how hungry the villagers may be after a long winter, they allow the first band of caribou that appears each spring to pass undisturbed. And the centuries-old survival prohibition against waste has been written into contemporary Gwich'in law: One should kill a caribou only when in need and then use as many parts of the animal as possible.

After a successful hunt, caribou meat is distributed in the community through a network of sharing, gift giving, and trade. The heads, a traditional delicacy, are usually roasted over an open fire. The meat is preserved by freezing or drying, and provides about 75 percent of the protein in the Gwich'in diet. Skins are sewn into slippers, purses, winter boots, bags, shirts, and other garments. Bones are fashioned into awls, hooks, handles, skin scrapers, and other tools. And the spirit of the caribou is honored in songs, stories, and dances.

In August 1990, the Gwich'in chiefs invited me up to Arctic Village to witness the affirmation of their tribal ties and their preparation for the battle to save the caribou calving grounds. During the week-long gathering, the evenings were filled with storytelling and feasting —caribou roasted over open fires. Around midnight, Chief Trimble Gilbert would get out his fiddle. Someone else would set up drums. Then everyone—from restless little preschool kids to the oldest women leaning on their willow walking sticks—would dance until dawn. Later in the day, people got down to the serious effort of preserving their culture. One by one, men and women asked for the diamond-willow talking stick, rose, and voiced their fears and hopes.

"My grandfather built caribou fences up in the mountains and was ready to defend them with his life," said Jonathan Soloman, resplendent in a caribou-leather vest that his wife had made and adorned with beads. "I was raised by my father out on the land. It was a good way of life. My father handed it down to me and I will hand it down to my children. The Gwich'in people will stand alone if we have to. It is time for us to say, 'This is ours, and we will defend it once and for all.'"

A very old man, whose deeply lined face peered out from under a baseball cap, took the stick. "Today we are living in two different worlds," he said, first in Gwich'in and then in English. "I live a traditional life of hunting and fishing. But look, I wear boots from Taiwan and jeans from the U.S. It's funny, but it's serious. We come from the land, like the caribou. They are our brothers. We have to defend their calving grounds. If I have to give my life to protect the calving grounds, I will."

Then Sarah James rose to speak. "Caribou are not just what we eat; they are who we are. They are in our stories and songs and the whole way we see the world. Caribou are our life. Without caribou we wouldn't exist."

Later, I visited Sarah in her two-room house, set on a knoll at the edge of Arctic Village. Clothes, books, canned goods, a hammer, and a hair dryer were stacked on the counter. In a corner stood a barrel of drinking water Sarah had hauled up from the river. The black hair hanging over Sarah's shoulders showed the first streaks of gray. As she bustled about the room making coffee, her face broke easily into a broad smile. When the coffee was ready, she sat for a few minutes to talk.

"You know, my father had a trapline a hundred miles from his nearest neighbor," she said, recalling how she and her seven brothers and sisters grew up on the Salmon River. "We had to work to survive. I helped with chores every day. I cut wood, snared rabbits, fished for grayling. Sometimes I'd go beaver snaring with my father, to help him and to learn the way. I never went to school until I was thirteen, but I learned from living out in the wilderness, our natural world. Right now I can survive in the government world. But I'd rather live in the natural world. It's a good life—fishing, hunting, gathering berries and roots.

"We never got bored. In the fall we had ice skating and fishing. In winter we played in snow drifts. And in the evenings my older brother, Gideon—he's chief at Venetie now— would read to us. We did a lot of carving, playing cards, and my dad would make snowshoes and toboggans and harnesses—everything that we

used. And we would help with that. Our mom— everything that we wore, she sewed. And she did the tanning, fur sewing, and beadwork."

Sarah had lit a Coleman stove to make the coffee. Today, the Gwich'in lifestyle also includes oil products—produced by the very industry they find themselves pitted against. Nearly everyone uses gasoline to run boats and snowmobiles. Most Gwich'in don't think of themselves as anti-oil. In fact, they once authorized oil exploration on some of their lands outside the range of the caribou.

"We learned a lot from dealing with those seismic crews looking for oil," said Sarah. "And we learned a lot from that *Exxon Valdez* oil spill. I don't think we'll be letting oil companies in here again. You see, we've still got clean air and water,

Sandy Hopson of Arctic Village dresses for a ceremonial dance in clothes and dancing slippers made from caribou hides.

and we want to keep it that way. There are places that shouldn't be disturbed for anything. Some places are too important, too special for the animals. The calving grounds must be left alone."

Nonsense, says British Petroleum geologist Roger Herrera. "The Gwich'in concerns are greatly exaggerated. It's inconceivable that development will cause a change greater than natural cyclic ones. Anyway, it's inevitable that these people will have to change."

But the Gwich'in resist the idea of being forced to change their way of life. As Sarah puts it, "We have been here for thousands of years. We know the weather, the animals, the vegetation, and the seasons. We are capable of living up here. And we want to educate our people as we once did, teaching our children. If others would only just respect our ways and our judgment."

The Gwich'in consider the oil industry's record at Prudhoe Bay solid reason to reject its proposed drilling in the Arctic National Wildlife Refuge. From 1973 to 1992 there were more than seventeen thousand oil spills at Prudhoe. Many of these were relatively small, but Prudhoe operations have also released thousands of tons of nitrogen oxides into the air each year, and disposal pits have frequently leaked arsenic, lead, and chromium. Some officials, such as John Turner, director of the U.S. Fish and Wildlife Service, have dismissed the significance of these problems, saying that "experiences at Prudhoe Bay provide a measure of assurance that caribou can coexist successfully with oil development." On the other hand, the Canadian government, which has no financial interest in Arctic Refuge development, pointed out that "disruption of caribou has already occurred in the vicinity of oil development. Calving has nearly ceased in the Prudhoe Bay oil field. Starving and dead caribou were documented near Nuiqsit, just west of the oil fields."

Caught between conflicting reports and assessments, the Gwich'in ask, Why take a chance? Why risk the caribou? Why gamble

with our culture? To fight the lobbying efforts of some of the world's largest multinational oil companies, the Gwich'in pooled their resources. It wasn't easy: With only a handful of cash-paying jobs in their villages, most families earn less than $5,000 a year. But as the showdown over Arctic drilling loomed in Congress, they managed to send Sarah James and Jonathan Soloman to Washington to testify.

The Gwich'in proposed the creation of a biocultural preserve to protect not only the caribou but also the ecosystems and native people on both sides of the Alaska-Canadian border. They also asked for wilderness status in the refuge, because "that is the only way to protect our culture from all the industrial pressure." Schooled as they are in surviving by wasting nothing, the Gwich'in pointed out that conservation measures, such as raising the fuel efficiency of cars just a mile or two per gallon, could save as much oil as that estimated to lie under the refuge. "They only expect to find enough oil to fuel America for about two hundred days," Sarah said. "Why risk our culture for two hundred days of oil?"

On February 19, 1992, after heated debate, the U.S. Senate passed a drastically modified energy bill. It provided only a few energy-saving measures and didn't even address the idea of a biocultural reserve. But the bill did block drilling in the Arctic Wildlife Refuge, at least temporarily. For this reprieve, there was rejoicing in Gwich'in villages. People sang, danced, offered prayers of thanks. In Canada, the village of Old Crow canceled school for the day.

The next time I saw Sarah, she was in Paris at a U.N.-sponsored gathering of community leaders from around the world. When it was her turn to speak, she looked out over the faces of a thousand people without saying a word. The great hall fell silent. When Sarah began speaking, she spoke in Gwich'in. Her words moved out over the packed auditorium in unfamiliar syllables, but I think everyone understood: Here was a woman far from home, speaking up for her people, who were proud to be who they were.

Then she switched to English. "We are the caribou people. We just won a battle to protect the caribou and our way of life. But we know the oil companies will come at us again. More battles lie ahead. Not just up there in Alaska, but all over. It will be hard. We have to work together. The Gwich'in are going to fight as long as we need to. We know that without the land we are nobody."

Amanda and Sophie Tritt of Arctic Village.

CREE

THE BATTLE OF JAMES BAY

The attitude of the dam builders has been, 'We'll build it and *then* we'll deal with the problems,'" said Kenneth Gilpin, chief of the Eastmain Cree in Quebec. "There is nothing they can give us that will justify this whole mess. They are destroying our way of life. That's the bottom line for the Cree. No amount of money is ever going to fix what they are taking away. It's really, really difficult for me to have to watch."

I met Gilpin during a three-day meeting of Cree chiefs in Val D'or, four hundred miles north of Montreal. Closeted behind closed doors, they tried to develop a strategy for fighting the largest hydroelectric project ever undertaken. If all three phases of the James Bay Project are completed, forty-seven dams and six hundred and sixty-seven dikes would divert twenty major rivers, convert an area of wild marshes twice the size of New York state into a system of artificial waterways, and threaten the ecological balance of an area the size of France. Gilpin's community had been hit hard by the first set of dams.

"The river was our main source of water," said Chief Gilpin. "You could go down there every morning, take your bucket, and bring fresh water up to your house for drinking. You can't do that anymore."

"You mean the river has dried up?" I asked.

"The river's not totally dry. It's like a little stream. We used to fish and trap on this river year round. Every morning in the summer, you'd see people out there in their canoes, checking out their nets. You don't see that anymore. All you see is brown, a brown river. Our elders wonder where all the deep water is. Well, it's not there anymore.

"A river disappearing is like a death. But you know, when a person dies, maybe it's your father that you loved so much, he dies and he's gone. And then life goes on. But when that river dies you've still got to look at it every day. That dry river bank—you can't get away from it. It's always there reminding you."

"How are your people responding to this?" I asked.

A Cree hunter of James Bay returns with geese.

"Are you asking if the Cree are mad? Of course we are mad," replied Chief Gilpin, who is slight of build but speaks forcefully. "But what has been done has been done. We just don't want other communities to suffer the way we have. Since the flooding of our lands, we've had more drinking and family problems. Just this last week, a girl went into a coma because of drinking. A drunk driver ran over a young kid out sledding. And there've been suicides. We try to explain these things to the government—"

"How does the government respond?"

"It doesn't. No response at all. Some of our young people are getting so angry they want to fight. But I tell them we've got to look at ourselves, to who we are as Cree. How do Cree solve problems? It's not by picking up arms. That's not going to solve anything.

"Our people understand that times are changing. But we still have to find ways to maintain our way of life, maintain our culture, our traditions. We're trying to prepare ourselves so we don't disappear."

❖

The government of Quebec had been quietly planning the massive James Bay Project for ten years before making a public announcement in the spring of 1971. Billy Diamond, now chief of the Wasaganish band, remembers the day he first heard the news.

"I was eighteen years old at the time," Diamond told me in a voice so deep it seemed to resonate from his barrel chest. "I remember getting up that morning and telling my wife, 'Well, I'm going hunting today.' I spent the day with my dad and it was really nice. He had been chief for fourteen years, and I couldn't have had a better teacher. If the community had a problem, they turned to Malcolm Diamond. He'd walk them through it. That day Dad and I went out about fifteen miles from the community. It was just getting dark when we got back. I came in

with five geese and my wife said to me, 'You better turn the radio on. They announced something about James Bay.' I tuned in the national news on CBC and they were talking about harnessing seven major rivers and constructing eleven large dams."

Billy Diamond and his friend Philip Washes started calling the Cree communities, saying, "We've got to do something." At the end of June 1971, the council of chiefs held their first strategy meeting. It was actually the first time in the Cree's history that all the Cree chiefs gathered together.

"These were all very strong men," Diamond said, "but we had this horrifying feeling of being helpless. We knew that we were coming up against a giant—Hydro Quebec. How could we fight this powerful corporation?

"But I remember my dad sitting down with me. I'll never forget this. He said, 'Listen, when you were young I knew you wanted to stay in our community, but I sent you away to school. I did it for one purpose—so you could learn the ways of the white man. Now you have to take what you learned, turn it around, and use it to our advantage. We didn't send you to school for nothin'. We knew something like this was coming. Now, you have the tools. Don't feel helpless. Don't say you don't have the resources. You *have* the resources.'

"And I looked around and I said, 'Dad, what are you talking about?'

"He said, 'The resources are the white man. That's the resource you use, the white man's law. You take the white man's law and you use it against him. You will find something in it.'"

Young Billy Diamond and Philip Washes tried to come up with a strategy. "At first, we had no ideas," said Diamond. "So we started looking into the laws. Asking questions. How did Quebec get this territory? If they didn't get it from us, they must have gotten it some other way, without our knowledge."

In a tent used as a communal kitchen, Cree women roast geese and bread over an open fire.

The Cree needed a lawyer, and in James O'Riley they found one ready to fight for their rights. "I have no money," Diamond told him. "The Cree have no money. We don't know when we can pay you. But I want you to be our lawyer for the James Bay court case."

A month later, O'Riley joined forces with the Cree, and they decided to take the offensive with their most vital issue—aboriginal rights. Canadian law had few legal precedents for recognizing native peoples' aboriginal rights to the freedoms of speech, religion, education, and so forth that others enjoy. Unlike native nations in the United States, Canadian natives had few treaties with their national government. Nevertheless, an eighty-year-old Quebec Boundaries Extension Act required the province of Quebec to settle native claims, an obligation it had never fulfilled. Before pressing this argument in court, the Cree

arranged a meeting with Quebec Premier Robert Bourassa to try to negotiate a settlement.

"That meeting with Bourassa was probably the most difficult experience of my life," said Diamond. "None of us younger leaders were asked to speak. The Cree elders had chosen one of their own. They said, 'It's going to be Malcolm Diamond who will speak. He'll speak to Bourassa. Everybody listens to Malcolm. Bourassa's got to listen to Malcolm.'

"My dad started speaking to Bourassa. But in the middle of my dad's speech Bourassa cut him off. Bourassa picked up his papers and said, 'I don't have time for this. I've got another meeting, another luncheon meeting.'

"There was silence. None of the guys wanted to look at me. And I couldn't look at my dad. The pain and the tears were starting to form in my heart and come up through my

move, alcoholism, drug use, domestic violence, and family breakups have all increased markedly. Some of these problems have been exacerbated by the intrusions of outsiders—the road to the hydro project made it much easier for hunters, tourists, and salesmen to reach their community.

"People come in and say, 'You should be like us,'" said Pachanos. "Hydro Quebec officials ask our people, 'Why do you want to live in the Stone Age?' But we need our language, our culture, our own identity. The biggest danger is wanting to live like everybody else. A lot of us with education are coming back to our communities. We are all struggling to find ways to join the best of our traditional life with the modern life. We have to do everything we can to maintain who we are."

❖

"The land is our provider, our healer, and our inspiration," Chief Billy Diamond told me over breakfast in a small cafe. "It's who we are. Every lake, every creek, every hill, every mountain ridge is a part of who we are. Without the land we would be nothing. To survive we must bring the young people onto the land."

"And if more land is flooded, what's going to happen to the people in villages like Great Whale?" I asked.

"This is my greatest fear," said Chief Diamond. "The people of Great Whale simply can't handle what's coming. Reality is going to crash down on them. They are quiet people, not very aggressive. This is going to overwhelm them. I hope I am wrong. But I don't think they can survive as a people if these new dams are built. They've been fighting as hard as they can, but they haven't made any preparations in case it is built."

He was silent for a moment, thinking deeply. Then he looked up and spoke with great directness. "I have to admit something to you. I've said this to a number of Crees and they don't like to hear it. But somebody has to say it. Those dams are probably going to be built. I know what Hydro Quebec is capable of doing. And Hydro Quebec and the government of Quebec have made up their minds to build those dams, even if it means the end of the Cree people."

"This must be hard to admit, even to yourself."

"Yes. It's heartbreaking to feel this way. It's even worse to talk to Crees about it."

❖

When the chiefs finished their last day of meetings at Val D'or, I sat down over dinner with Robbie Niquanicappo. He had just been appointed acting chief of the Whapmagoostui band of Great Whale, which stands to lose most of its land if the next series of dams is built. I asked him how it feels to be Cree in this time.

"I want to live as our ancestors did," said Robbie, a large, well-built man with a surprisingly soft voice. "I want to be able to go out on the land to hunt and fish, to enjoy the things my ancestors enjoyed."

"How will you pass on your way of life to your children?" I asked.

"We have our ways," said Robbie. "You see, as a Cree man, you usually don't tell your son, 'Go split some wood for me.' You go out and do it yourself. You let your kids watch you. We call it shadowing, and this spring I'll be starting it with my five-year-old son. When I take him out trapping with me, I'm not going to tell him what to do, just let him observe so he can see what it's all about. In this way, he'll learn how to work and to love the land. As we take more trips together, the land will become a part of him.

"I remember going out with my father. And later, when I got out of school, I came straight home. You know, I was born in camp in 1958, and I can take my family to that very spot and say, 'My mother's head rested here. Here's where I first hit the ground, right at this point.' I know it may be hard for others to understand, but when we talk about going home, we don't mean to a house. The land is our home."

"And you'll pass this feeling on to your children?"

"Oh, yeah. In lots of ways. Like early in the spring, we'll start talking about the goose hunt. I'll go out to my camp with my son just for the joy of getting ready. It's along the bay, a spot that I share with my uncle. A lot of the older men do that, they'll invite a young hunter to share a spot. When my uncle passes away, I'll still be able to camp there with my family. Nobody owns it. I mean, anybody else can come in there who wants to. Anyone's perfectly welcome. That's the way it is. Nobody owns the land."

"But doesn't the government think it's their land?" I asked.

"Sure, the government people think they own it, but they don't even *know* the land," said Robbie. "If they had any idea what wonderful country this was, they wouldn't think about flooding it. Eighty-seven percent of the good land around my village is going to be lost— 87 percent. This isn't easy to live with."

"Do you think the rest of the dams are going to be built?" I asked. "How do you deal with that possibility?"

"Let's put it this way," said Robbie. "It's not going to happen in my lifetime. And if it does. . . ." He paused and looked away for several seconds. "The moment that first spadeful of dirt is thrown, that's our death sentence. Forget it. The Crees aren't going to be able to survive something like that. We may survive physically. You might see us walking around, but we'll be a people without an identity. A people without a link to our past. Probably a very lost people."

Cree children of James Bay. "Please don't view us as Hollywood Indians," says Robbie Niquanicappo of Great Whale. "I don't like the noble savage image. Just see us as people who are trying to stay alive, save the land for our children, for all children."

THE STRUGGLE FOR RELIGIOUS FREEDOM

*A*rt, would you like to come pray with us for four days?" asked Pat Locke on a cold January day in 1992. I couldn't remember the last time I had been invited to pray with a family, let alone for four days.

"Our Sun Dance will be in July," said Pat. "We'll fast with the dancers for four days and help them pray. We'll be praying for other people and for the earth."

I felt honored to be invited and told Pat I'd be there. For at least nineteen generations, the Sun Dance has been one of the most sacred rites of the Lakota, but for most of this century it's been banned by the U.S. government. Although the Sun Dance is legal once again, the First Amendment's freedom-of-religion clause has never worked well for American Indians, and many of them are still struggling for the right to worship that most of us take for granted.

In mid-July, I flew to South Dakota, rented a car, and drove to one of the isolated Lakota reservations. I left behind the flat patchwork cornfields and entered the rolling grasslands where vast herds of buffalo once grazed. Twenty-three years earlier, Pat's family and mine had shared a house on a mountainside near Anchorage. Our children had wandered in and out of each other's kitchens and living rooms. The night my second son was born, Pat had driven my wife to the hospital. Later, after the Lockes had moved from Alaska, Pat's son Kevin had come back up to stay with me one summer. The family is Hunkpapa Lakota and had eventually come back to this South Dakota country where their ancestors had lived.

The homes of Winona and Kevin, Pat's children, stand on the highest point of land for many miles. "This is the meaning of the sacred hoop of life," said Pat, turning round with me there to look in every direction. Running north and south is the red road, the good and straight way: The south is the source of life, and to the north is purity. The blue or black road of destruction and error runs east and west. Black Elk, the great Lakota visionary, once said, "He who travels on this path is distracted, is ruled by his senses and lives for himself rather than his people."

On this day, a blistering sun hung in the sky and shadows of clouds drifted over the land. Yellow butterflies fluttered in the grass, meadowlarks in the sky. One meadowlark hopped toward me, coming so close that I could see each yellow feather on its chest and the flecks of gray etched on its wings and back. A hawk swooped by in a long graceful arc, alighted on a rock, stood still as a rock itself, and then lifted lightly into the air, gliding away over the rim of a hill. Pat pointed to a distant butte, where medicine men would take young men on vision quests—four days of fasting and praying to receive a vision from God. How rare it is for most of us to be alone in nature for even a single day. And if we do leave the busyness of our daily lives for an extended period, who is there on our return to help us understand what we saw, felt, or dreamed?

Several miles out, a twister wandered over the long green hills. Earth and sky joined in this wild funnel of wind, which swirled dust hundreds of feet in the air. When the dust settled back to earth, the sky was clear again all the way out to Bear Butte, where Crazy Horse used to camp.

"As generations come and go, some change is natural. Evolution is a part of life," said Pat. "But we must resist the sudden intrusive changes that are imposed upon us. As indigenous people, we have to articulate what we mean by change, define what we perceive as essential to our way of life. We have to refuse to accept blindly others' perceptions of progress. Just as our people were warriors in the past, so must we be warriors on this new battlefield, fighting all these forced changes to our way of life."

At dusk, Pat's extended family and several friends walked down to the shore of a nearby river. We gathered driftwood logs, lit a fire, and laid some good-sized rocks in the heart of the flames. After the rocks had baked for about an hour, they were carried into the sweat lodge, made of pieces of canvas and carpet stretched over a bent-willow frame. This sweat would purify us before the Sun Dance. "*Mitaku ye oya sin* (we are all related)," we said as we entered the sweat lodge. With the flap closed, it was completely dark. We prayed and sang.

"I want to give thanks to the people who saved these songs," said one of the men. "Around the turn of the century, about six men made sure these songs survived. Some of the old men I've taken sweats with would just sing, song after song. All their thanksgiving was in their songs."

The next day we drove on back roads deep into the reservation and came at length to the lush meadows and stands of cottonwood trees where the Sun Dance would be held. The Sun Dance is one of the seven ceremonies that the White Buffalo Calf Woman, a Messenger of God, brought to the Lakota people. Black Elk tells us that when the White Buffalo Calf Woman came nineteen generations ago, she said, "With this sacred Pipe you will walk upon the Earth, for the Earth is your Grandmother and Mother, and She is sacred. Every step taken upon her should be as a prayer . . . and you must always remember

Patricia Locke, Lakota. "From Point Barrow to Tierra del Fuego, we are still fighting for our survival and human rights, especially that most fundamental of human rights, freedom of religion."

that the two-leggeds and all the other peoples who stand upon this earth are sacred and should be treated as such."

The first night, I was asked to be a fire keeper. It was my job to stay up and keep the fire burning throughout the night. Overhead, the clear, black sky was lit with stars, and a cool breeze blew in from the north. A thunderstorm intermittently lit the northern horizon along hundreds of miles, sometimes glowing red in the clouds, sometimes streaking the sky with quick, blue-white flashes of light. Now and then, the crack and low rumbling of thunder rolled in from afar, momentarily overwhelming the sound of crickets in the grass.

Alone with my thoughts and the fire, I gazed from flames to stars, from one to the other, hour after hour. Early in the morning, still an hour or two before the dawn, coyotes called across the darkened prairie. Members of the same pack, it seemed, were hunting apart, some by the river, others high on the hill. Their howling and quick yelps rose and fell and lingered in the darkness.

In more than thirty years of going to wild places, I've treasured every night spent out under the turning of stars, every night feeling the force of wind and snow. But this night was different. It wasn't just the coyotes, the stars, and the fire, but how this time of reverence drew them together with the sleeping dancers, their families, and the prairie stretching into the night in all directions.

With the first pale light, the dancers awoke. Over the next four days, they danced and prayed. And we prayed with them. Because of the sacred nature of this time of prayer, no photographs or sketches were allowed. In this same spirit, the details of what I saw, shared, and experienced will not enter this writing, but will remain there in that sacred space by the cottonwood trees under that enormous sky.

As the Sun Dance drew to a close, I walked alone for a while among the clumps of sage and tall grass, feeling peaceful but troubled. How could something as beautiful and sacred as this prayer gathering ever have been illegal in the United States? Like most Americans, I had grown up believing that no matter what the color of our skin, rich or poor, all of us at least have the right to worship as we wish.

It is said that the reason the Sun Dance was banned in the late 1800s was that a cavalry officer's wife found it too painful and fainted from the sight. It does physically test the dancers mightily, but after seven or so centuries of Sun Dancing, the Lakota hardly needed to be protected from themselves. Many of them believe that the government had a hidden reason for banning their dance. "The real reason," one elder explained, "was to break our Lakota social fabric, our organization, our cohesiveness. Even powwows were outlawed. No one under forty was allowed to dance."

In the 1930s, Oscar Henry One Bull, who had been raised by Sitting Bull, pleaded with the government, "Our world is in such turmoil. We long to have our prayers once again. We need an infusion of spirit." One dance was permitted in 1936; thereafter, it remained illegal.

The Sun Dance had a profound impact on me. It is one thing to know that Lakota spirituality is as complex as Hinduism and that the White Buffalo Calf Woman is regarded as a Messenger from the Creator, much as Mohammed and Jesus are for other peoples. But it was only through experiencing those four days in a remote corner of a Lakota reservation that I could begin to understand, *really* understand, how incredibly cruel has been the U.S. government's suppression of the Sun Dance and other American Indian religious practices.

❖

The suppression of indigenous spirituality is hardly confined to the United States. On December 10, 1992, indigenous leaders from more than fifty countries told the United Nations that "governments continue to desecrate and appropriate religious and sacred places and objects, depriving indigenous nations around the world of their basic spiritual ways of life."

In one country after another, native religious problems have long arisen with great frequency. Sacred sites have been lost or destroyed. Overzealous missionaries have cast traditional medicine men and women as devils, sometimes killing them in the name of the Christian faith. Religious objects have been confiscated, destroyed, placed in museums, and sold as artifacts. Languages have slipped away, and with them sacred songs and peoples' ways of praying.

Many of the obstacles to religious freedom have arisen from the inherent conflicts between the values and the world view of indigenous peoples and those of the dominant society. While technological people value saving and acquiring, indigenous people value sharing and giving. In Western cultures, spirituality is usually separated from the rest of life; in native cultures it is integrated with daily living. Technological societies tend to adopt the concept of a single, paternalistically defined God or else incline toward atheism.

Indigenous peoples often find that the mainstream culture tries to undermine the creation liturgies that define their fundamental relationships with their Creator. Anthropologists have unearthed old campfires and burial sites to build a theoretical trail of evidence that traces the origin of American Indians back over the Bering land bridge to Asia. But despite the archaeological data, there were no Lakota or Apache in Asia. The Yup'ik never lived there and neither did the Cree. By their very nature, indigenous peoples are of the land that lives in their songs and oral histories. They are peoples born of specific places on the land. The essence of their being has been shaped by the winds, rivers, seas, mountains, and plains where they dwell.

Not surprisingly, most indigenous peoples have grown ever more protective of their spiritual beliefs. Many have had to worship in secrecy, and recently have had to go to court to try to regain their right to worship in the manner of their ancestors.

In 1978, the U.S. Congress passed the American Indian Religious Freedom Act. Its intent was "to protect and preserve for American Indians their inherent right of freedom to believe, express, and exercise the traditional religions . . . including but not limited to access to sites, use and possession of sacred objects, and the freedom to worship through ceremonials and traditional rites."

While this act finally legalized the Sun Dance and other sacred ceremonies, it fell well short of protecting the religious freedom of American Indians. The Lakota, for example, face an ongoing struggle to protect their sacred ceremonial pipes and the stone from which they are made. For centuries, Plains Indians have journeyed from afar to reach the one site in Minnesota where the stone is found. Like all things sacred, the pipestone must be treated with reverence. Arvol Looking Horse, who is the nineteenth caretaker of the Pipe that the White Buffalo Calf Woman brought to the Lakota, insists that pipestone and objects made from pipestone must never be sold. "We must not play with the Pipe," he says. "It is our life."

Pete Catches, a Lakota holy man, says, "Pipestone, both below and above the ground, is sacred. It is the blood of our people."

Nevertheless, the National Park Service authorizes the sale of pipestone paraphernalia in gift shops at Pipestone National Monument. The Dakota Lakota and Cheyenne have made repeated appeals to halt these sales. And each spring, people of the Indian nations make a six-week journey on foot to protest commercial exploitation of this sacred stone. Still, every day in the monument's gift shop, pipestone pipes, trinkets, and ashtrays are sold to tourists, who have no idea of the sacred nature of the stone.

For ten years, from 1978 to 1988, American Indians enjoyed the same fundamental human right to religious freedom that all American citizens enjoy. In 1988, however, the Religious Freedom Act was emasculated in a crucial test— the Lyng case. The underlying controversy arose when the U.S. Forest Service decided to build a road through the Six Rivers National Forest in

In December 1990, three hundred Lakota made a two-hundred-mile ride in minus fifty-degree temperatures to commemorate the Wounded Knee Massacre of 1890. The lead rider, Arvol Looking Horse, carries a staff decorated with eagle feathers honoring dead warriors. The five-day ride, during which some fasted and others dressed in rags, was both a memorial and a rite of healing after a century of grieving.

northern California. The government wanted to improve access for logging trucks. But the new road would cut through a secluded area of woods that the Yurok, Karok, and Tolowa call the "High Country."

For centuries, the religious leaders of these nations assembled at this site every year to conduct ceremonies for the renewal of the world. Now they faced the prospect of twenty-ton trucks loaded with redwood logs rumbling through their secluded and sacred forest. How, they asked, could the very place where they prayed for the renewal of the earth be used to facilitate destruction of a forest?

The three Indian nations filed a lawsuit, and after considerable legal pressure, the Forest Service canceled the ill-conceived road. However, the legal arguments over the government's trust responsibilities to American Indians worked their

way up to the U.S. Supreme Court. On April 19, 1988, Justice Sandra Day O'Conner acknowledged that there was "no reason to doubt that the logging and road-building projects at issue in this case could have devastating effects on traditional Indian religious practices."

Nevertheless, O'Conner and a one-vote majority of the justices ruled that when a choice must be made between unconstitutional prohibition of religious freedom and the government's conduct of its affairs, the decision "cannot depend on measuring the effects of a governmental action on a religious objector's spiritual development."

In other words, the Supreme Court ruled that government land rights take precedence over the religious rights of American Indians. The American Indian Religious Freedom Act does not specifically restrict the government's use of its lands—even if the government's actions infringe upon or destroy a religion. This ruling held that even religious ceremonies that have been practiced for thousands of years could not interfere with the government's use of federal lands.

The Lyng ruling effectively stripped American Indians of protection, in both the American Constitution and federal courts, for their religious practices. Said Justice Brennan, "Today's ruling sacrifices a religion at least as old as the Nation itself, . . . so that the Forest Service can build a six-mile segment of a road that two lower courts found had only most marginal and speculative utility. . . . Given today's ruling, [the Indians' freedom to maintain their religious beliefs] amounts to nothing more than the right to believe that their religion will be destroyed."

While most Americans remained completely unaware of the Lyng decision, American Indians rallied to protect their sacred sites and ceremonies. In 1991 alone, more than twenty Indian nations lodged protests.

In Montana, the Salish and Kootenai nations asked for protection for Medicine Tree, a spiritual site used for healing and other religious purposes. But the state of Montana wanted to build a road through Medicine Tree and several other sacred sites. The Lyng decision effectively disarmed the Salish and Kootenai before they ever got to court.

In the Pacific Northwest, the Nez Percé have asked for special legislation to halt the excavation of "artifacts" from their oldest cultural sites. To their anguish, graves of their ancestors are being dug up and the personal items sold in European and Asian markets. Criminal statutes in all fifty states prohibit the desecration of graves, yet museums, government agencies, and private collectors warehouse the bodies of more than three hundred thousand American Indians. Where grave digging occurs on federal lands, the Lyng decision has left Indians virtually powerless to stop it.

In the Southwest, the people of the Taos Pueblo have asked for protection from the U.S. Air Force, whose planes fly as low as one hundred feet from the ground. An independent impact study found that the low-altitude flights did "disrupt traditional ceremonialism, intruding aurally or visually on meditation such as vision quests, which require solitude and isolation from man-made noises. . . . In cases of once in a lifetime ceremonies, interruption may result in irrevocable cancellation." In response, the Air Force ignored Taos tribal sovereignty and proclaimed that tribal air space is within the public domain, and, as such, indistinguishable from other public lands. The protests of the Taos people will be compromised by the Lyng decision.

In Arizona, the Lyng decision undermines the San Carlos Apache, who are fighting the construction of a major telescope on their sacred mountain, Dzil Nchaa si an (Mt. Graham). "This mountain is essential to the continued practice of physical and spiritual healing by Apache medicine men and women," says the San Carlos Apache Tribal Council. "The proposed destruction of this mountain will contribute directly to the destruction of fundamental aspects of traditional Apache spiritual life."

The Apache are not amused by the irony that the telescope, which is sponsored by the Vatican, has been named Columbus. "It really bothers us, especially our traditional people," Michael Davis of the Apache Survival Coalition told me. "Our whole tribe opposes the project—the tribal council, the traditional spiritual leaders, everyone."

I met Davis in the winter of 1992, when he and his wife, Ola, were at United Nations Headquarters in New York to protest the desecration of their mountain. "Some people don't view a telescope as the worst thing in the world," I said, playing the devil's advocate. "It's quiet, it doesn't pollute. Why does it trouble you so much?"

"Because the whole mountain is sacred. It's the most sacred place we have," Davis said. "A telescope and the people who come with it interfere with ceremonial activities. The mountain must remain just the way it is."

"Do your people still go up there?"

"Our medicine men go there to gather herbs and spring water. We have ceremonies on the mountain. And in the summer, families go up there to meditate, to be at peace with the mountain and themselves. We need to be able to go there and pray. Why is it so hard for others to understand that our religion is tied directly to the land?"

❖

Why *is* it so difficult for those of us who are not indigenous to grasp this spiritual connection to the land?

We wouldn't tolerate someone putting a telescope on top of one of our churches, temples, or mosques. Yet we act with indifference to the desecration of a sacred place built not of brick and mortar but of grass and trees. Are we so accustomed to praying with a roof over our heads that we can't conceive of worshiping at an open-air altar? Or are we simply too busy with our jobs, hobbies, and favorite television shows to develop all but the most superficial relationship with the land?

Of course, there was a time when we all shared a common spiritual link to the earth. If we look back far enough, we find that we are all descended from indigenous peoples. Each of us has tribal ancestors, who had their own sacred songs and dances; who were aided in their journeys through the circle of life by rites of passage, elders, and spiritual mentors; who lived in deep connection with the natural world. This awareness of ourselves as indivisible parts of nature is our common heritage, a belief system that has enabled us to survive for most of our time on earth. Only recently has civilization taken us on a disastrous detour.

I remember my father telling me, when I was very young, that Indians had a trick to keep from getting lost. He said that every now and then, they'd look back over their shoulder to see where they were coming from. Perhaps it's time for us all to look back over the way we've come.

When modern men and women first emerged, they lived as hunter-gatherers in small nomadic groups. About ten thousand years ago, some people began taking the first tentative steps that would gradually diminish their spiritual links to the land. They began farming. As they built the first crude fences to keep wild animals out and tame ones in, unwittingly they were building an invisible wall between themselves and the natural world. Instead of living with all their senses attuned to the sights, smells, sounds, and essences of the forest, plains, and sea, they began to shelter and guard themselves from the vagaries of nature. Generation by generation, they became more sedentary and gathered more possessions. And as they turned the soil, they developed the idea of owning and selling land. The growth of modern civilizations about five thousand years ago accelerated the movement of people to towns and cities, away from a more intimate and sacred connection with nature.

Through the ages of exploration and industrialization, and now in the age of technology, this rift between "indigenous" and "nonindigenous" world views has widened. These fundamentally different ways of perceiving the world are both present in our time. I think of how they appear in the families of my Yup'ik friend Harold Napoleon and myself. To Harold's great-grandfather, Apouluq, one of the most powerful shamans on the Bering Sea coast, the land, rivers, heavens, seas, and all that dwelled within them were spiritual—and therefore sacred. I remember Harold saying that "when Apouluq walked out into the tundra or launched his kayak, he entered the spiritual realm."

My great-grandfather, on the other hand, came west herding sheep when he was fourteen and helped "build the country." To J. P. Curry, land was to be improved, used to its fullest extent, bought, sold, leased, mortgaged, and, in the end, willed to progeny. And this was *my* inheritance—not just the land, but the unexamined belief that land is there to be developed, bought, and sold. It might be valued and even loved, but it was never considered sacred.

Fortunately, my family had a strong sense

of place. I knew my great-grandfather's homestead and spent many hours among the towering cottonwood trees that he had planted as a young man. I knew where the mourning doves liked to nest in spring and where the pheasants hid in fall. But today most of us live far from the places of our childhood dreaming.

"We should know that the Great Spirit is within all things: the trees, the grasses, the rivers, the mountains, all the four-legged animals, and the winged peoples," said Black Elk.

But how do we get to know, really *know* and experience this in our time? In modern America, we are so mobile that it's difficult to develop a deep relationship with the natural world. It's even hard to hold onto whatever relationship we had with the land as children or in the last place we lived. With two out of every five American families moving every year, it's difficult to develop a sense of place at all.

Without a connection to the land, our lives can quickly fall out of balance with the rest of nature. I remember hearing the Hopi elder Thomas Banyaca explain how the Creator made the first world in perfect balance. In 1948, all the traditional Hopi leaders met and selected four people to carry their message. The only surviving messenger is Banyaca, now in his seventies, silver-haired but still possessed of a youthful intensity. He tells us that in the first world humans turned away from moral and spiritual principles. They misused their spiritual powers for selfish purposes. That world was destroyed. Banyaca sees us approaching a similar crossroads today.

"The traditional Hopi follows the spiritual path that was given to us by Massau'u, the Great spirit," says Banyaca. "We made a sacred covenant to follow His life plan at all times, which includes the responsibility of taking care of this land. We have never made any treaties with any foreign nation, including the United States, but for many centuries we have honored this sacred agreement. Our goals are not to gain political control, monetary wealth, or military power, but rather to pray and to promote the welfare of all living beings and to preserve the world in a natural way. . . . The Hopi prophecy says that if we humans don't wake up to the warnings, the great purification will come to destroy this world, just as the previous worlds were destroyed."

Whether we listen to Hopi prophecy or the turmoil reported every evening on the news, I think we can find ample reason to turn toward a more respectful and sacred view of our world. And we need to address the religious rights of Native Americans—American Indians, Alaska Natives, Native Hawaiians, and Native Pacific Islanders. How can we go on compromising their religious freedom for the sake of ill-placed telescopes and pipestone ashtrays? Their survival as indigenous peoples requires religious freedom. So why not make sure that the Native American Religious Freedom Act has the strength to do what it is supposed to do? Why not permanently, once and forever, set aside their sacred sites? Why not return their religious objects and allow them to worship as they always have?

Before the time of the Sun Dance came around again, Native Americans mounted a fight for their spiritual freedom. My friend Pat Locke was asked to coordinate the coalition of seventy-four tribes and organizations seeking to amend the American Indian Religious Freedom Act—to put some teeth in it. When Pat moved to Washington, D.C., to fight for religious freedom in the halls of Congress, I knew she would miss her six grandchildren and the meadowlarks back home in South Dakota. I remember standing with her there in the midst of Sitting Bull's country, in the center of the hoop of life, when she reminded me that "some of our guests have forgotten that they came to our Turtle Island [North America] seeking a haven from religious persecution. Others seem not to realize that Tunkashala Wakan Tanka [God] so loved us, too, that many Messengers were sent to the red peoples of this hemisphere to teach us how to worship the one Great Spirit. As Pete Catches says, 'We are the beautiful colors of the flowers in the Creator's garden. God loves all the colors.'"

Safeguarding the religious freedom of Native Americans may be even more important for the rest of us, who are not indigenous and who need to begin making decisions out of respect for the earth. Oscar Henry One Bull might well have been pleading for us all when he sought "an infusion of spirit."

How might our world be different if our vision of the sacred embraced the earth? If more of us felt indigenous to wherever we live? If we took a little more time to notice the meadowlarks and butterflies, the thunder in the distance, and crickets in the grass?

"The resurrection of buried realities, the appearance of what was forgotten and repressed," writes Octavio Paz, "can lead, as it has in other times in history, to regeneration." The resurrection of indigenous realities has never been more timely. Still, we should resist trying to adopt or co-opt the sacred ceremonies of others, which are grounded in their language and their evolution as a people. And we shouldn't have to go to a Sun Dance to learn how to pray with our people for the well-being of all living things.

There is no turning back to the time of Black Elk and Apouluq. But if we continue on in the absence of the sacred, life as we know it will not survive.

A ceremonial meal is prepared for the medicine man during the four-day Apache Sunrise Ceremony, in which girls are "sung" into womanhood.

CENTRAL AMERICA

A NET MADE OF HOLES

W hen the Spanish conquistadors arrived in present-day Central America, they encountered people different from any they had ever seen. Distinct as these tribes were, they belonged to essentially one vast Mesoamerican culture, which extended from the Aztec empire of Mexico through the Mayan civilization of Guatemala and Honduras. In pre-Hispanic times, these people had built cities and religious centers and created extraordinary forms of literature, music, and art. Less than fifty years after the arrival of the first Europeans, their civilization would lie in ruins. The seeds of their current struggle for land, sovereignty, self-respect, and cultural identity were sown in that invasion five hundred years ago.

"In the beginning the Indians regarded the Spaniards as angels from Heaven," wrote Bartolome de Las Casas, a Spanish priest who witnessed the first decades of the invasion. He observed that "these Indians were by nature very gentle and peace-loving," and that "only after the Spaniards had used violence against them, killing, robbing, torturing, did the Indians ever rise up."

Five hundred years later, it is all but impossible to imagine the horror of the Conquest. One of the few surviving accounts comes from an anonymous Indian of Tlatelolco, who wrote in 1528:

> Broken spears lie in the roads.
> We have torn our hair in our grief.
> The houses are roofless now,
> and their walls are red with blood.
> The water has turned red,
> and it has the taste of brine.
> We have pounded our hands in despair
> against the adobe walls,
> for our inheritance was only
> a net made of holes.

A Lancandon Indian girl in Mexico.

Previous page: A village on the bank of the Amazon.

This net made of holes has been handed from generation to generation to the thirteen million indigenous people now living in Central America. Much like the Great Death in Alaska, the Conquest marked the psyche of the survivors and their descendants.

Some Central American cultures have already vanished. In Mexico alone, at least one hundred and thirteen languages have been extinguished. Other people have been assimilated and some have floundered, generation to generation, in a cultural wasteland, their traditional values and ways of living discarded and the ways of the new culture not yet assumed. Still others were determined to preserve their indigenous identity. The Yaquis in Sonora, for example, remained in a state of war with the Mexican government for many years, laying down their arms only when their ancestral lands and rights as a culturally distinct society were finally recognized.

Five centuries later, the majority of the indigenous peoples of Central America continue to resist the Conquest in its modern-day guise—repressive regimes and the long reach of multi-national corporations. Indigenous peoples have developed new forms of cultural, social, political, and sometimes armed resistance, and have sought alliances with poor nonnative Ladinos. The Ladino elite, with the support of their northern friends, respond with new and old forms of repression: death squads, "disappearances," torture and mutilation, massacres, ethnic genocide, "model" villages, forced recruitment into the military, and civil defense patrols. The civil wars in Central America, and especially that in Guatemala, are viewed by indigenous peoples as a continuation of the Conquest.

❖

To the casual visitor, Guatemala is a land of beautiful beaches, picturesque landscapes, and a pleasant climate. But behind this bucolic exterior is a de facto apartheid society. Ladinos, the ruling minority, control the economy, military, and political establishment, and consume most of the country's resources to support their fortified luxury. The Indians of Guatemala, the majority, have had most of their land stolen, are forced to provide their labor at survival wages, and are repressed by the state whenever they attempt to exercise their economic, political, and cultural rights.

"Many of my people are displaced. For them it is a matter of survival," Father José Angel Zapeta told me. He is a Quiché Indian and a Catholic priest. For the past fifteen years he has tried to bring relief to the dispossessed people of Guatemala. Looking at me with weary eyes, he said, "Many of our Indian people end up in the cities, where they face extreme poverty. Indians know how to live in the villages, but not in the cities. Men end up selling brooms and papers or shining shoes and gathering bottles. Teenage girls, who were once very shy and traditional, become prostitutes to buy food for their younger brothers and sisters.

"Your culture is your life," Father Zapeta said. "But if you are persecuted long enough, your culture suffers, gets lost."

Father Zapeta is himself a survivor of the four decades of terror and hidden violence that have ripped Guatemala apart. While tourists lolled on coastal beaches, Indians in the highlands were being thrown from their homes and murdered. For many years, most Americans, myself included, remained blissfully unaware of the atrocities committed in Central America—and of our own country's complicity. Today, nearly half of the indigenous people in Central America belong to the twenty-three tribal groups in Guatemala. Their persecution began long ago.

Within sixteen years of their arrival, the Spanish eliminated an estimated four million native Guatemalans. Many of those who survived became indentured to the Spaniards who had taken their lands. To this day, many Indians pay rent for small plots, plant fields, herd cattle, and surrender part of their production to the landowners. If they object to the working conditions or are unable to pay the rent, they are routinely

Kuna Indian women, Panama.

evicted from the land, even though their families may have lived on it for generations.

A revolution in 1944 resulted in the election of Jacobo Arbenz, who began returning land to the Guatemalan people. In a bold move, he expropriated some of the holdings of the United Fruit Company, which had controlled Guatemala's banana, cocoa, and coffee trade since 1871. At the time, John Foster Dulles was the U.S. Secretary of State, and his brother, Allen, directed the CIA. Both were former partners in the United Fruit Company's law firm. The U.S. government decided that Arbenz's reforms posed a Socialist threat to American interests.

In 1954, the CIA organized a coup that overthrew the Arbenz government and began Guatemala's forty years of unremitting terror. The new regime systematically massacred Indians

to get their lands; the first to suffer were those to whom United Fruit lands had been distributed. Since that CIA-backed military coup, more than one hundred and fifty thousand Indians have been killed and some seventy thousand families have lost their lands.

The succession of military dictatorships following the coup led to the growth of armed revolutionary movements and a thirty-three-year civil war. Indigenous people's support and participation in the Western Highlands guerrilla insurgency from the late 1970s to this day have led to violent repression against Indian communities.

In 1981, the army initiated an eighteen-month "scorched earth" campaign that destroyed four hundred and forty Indian villages. The destruction of the village of San Francisco, in Huehuetenango, was typical. Soldiers pulled the men to one side and locked up women and children in a church. Then they shot the men. A survivor recalled that "the soldiers began to fire at the women inside the church. The majority did not die there but were separated from their children, taken to their homes, and killed, apparently with machetes. . . . Then the soldiers returned to kill the children."

Three hundred and fifty-two people died that day in San Francisco. Altogether, the scorched earth campaign made orphans of more than two hundred thousand children. Entire communities disappeared. A million people became refugees in their own country; another two hundred thousand escaped to Mexico.

A particularly bitter irony for the Indian people is knowing that many of the soldiers who terrorize their villages are indoctrinated Indians. On festival or market days, military trucks arrive to round up young Indian men, whether or not they want to be recruited. One fourteen-year-old, whose name must remain secret, has described how he was forced to fight his own people. One day, recruiters grabbed him from the street, threw him into a truck, and took him to the Honor Guard Base in Guatemala City.

"Some things are very difficult to talk about," he said. "As part of the training, we were taken to the torture center to show us how to do it. They used a wire heated in fire to burn

Mothers of "Heroes and Martyrs" demonstrate for peace with pictures of their sons killed in Nicaragua.

people's arms. They cut off ears, arms, and legs, cut out their tongues. They told us that if we talked about these things, they would know we were Communists and kill us. They gave us a full glass of dog blood every three days, and sent us out to kill people. There is something in the dog blood that gives you the overwhelming desire to kill. The desire is so strong you really don't even care if you are killing a child."

After six months of training, the recruit was sent into the jungle to fight Indian guerrillas. He had seen friends shot when they tried to escape. Nevertheless, one rainy afternoon he decided to make a run for it. He threw himself into a river and, when the soldiers started shooting, tried to keep his head underwater. As darkness fell, the soldiers gave up tracking him, and he threw off his clothes and ran through the forest.

"I ran until I came to a little shack. There was a woman who let me in and told me to wait there. A little while later she came back with new shoes, pants, and a shirt. I told her who I was and what I had done and asked her why she was helping me. She said, 'I know who you are, and I'm giving you these things because you saved yourself from a very great evil.'"

From afar, it is often difficult to perceive how profoundly the United States can shape events like these in Guatemala. "The fruits of those interventions have been veiled in a vast shroud of silence in the U.S. press and public domain," writes Susanne Jonas in *The Battle for Guatemala*. "At the human level, it is a tale of wholesale slaughter and genocide. . . . That this holocaust was almost unknown and unimagined in most Western countries, certainly in the United States, is a testament to the 'great silence' about Guatemala—an indifferent, at times complicitous silence, perhaps because the victims were overwhelmingly Indians."

The shadow of U.S. involvement in Guatemala is long. All senior officers in the Guatemalan army, the institution responsible for the massacres, have received training in the United States. When military aid was finally cut off under President Carter because of human rights violations, Israel stepped in as the main source of military aid and training of the Guatemalan military. Even though human rights abuses continued during the 1980s, the Reagan and Bush administrations resumed limited military sales, training, and aid. In short, one administration after another has justified various forms of intervention by claiming to promote democracy by opposing the spread of communism. Ironically, communism has pretty well taken care of its own demise, and U.S. manipulation of elections has undermined the democratic process and increased social inequities.

Today, a great disparity between rich and poor is seen everywhere in Central America, but nowhere is it more extreme than in Guatemala. Only 13 percent of the population live above the poverty level. Two percent of the people now own 70 percent of Guatemala's usable land. Eighty percent of the farmers own only 10 percent of the land. And the grip of poverty is tightening. In the 1980s, unemployment increased 600 percent, and only one in five adults could find a job. In 1987, UNICEF reported that "Guatemala has the worst illiteracy rate in Central America, the highest number of infants with low birth weight, and the lowest percentage of pupils enrolled in school."

By virtually all indicators, the indigenous majority has borne the brunt of this inequity. Life expectancy for Indians is sixteen years lower than for Ladinos. Sixty-one percent of the Indians are illiterate, compared with 29 percent of Ladinos; in some mountain regions 85 percent of the indigenous women are illiterate. The infant mortality rate is twice the national average. And more than a million Indians remain refugees.

It may be impossible for those of us in the developed world who have homes and jobs to understand how it feels to be an indigenous refugee—homeless, deprived of human rights, haunted by the memory of loved ones lost or killed, each day struggling to find something to eat, and never free from the threat of violence. Paramilitary death squads have so thoroughly terrorized local people that some deny their Indian identity in order to survive.

Even priests have no immunity. Many of those who have tried to assist Indians have been forced to flee the country. Fourteen of those, who like Father Zapeta stayed to help, have been killed. "The hardest thing for me to see is the breaking up of families. Those that suffer most are those without men or boys. Life is especially hard for the older women. They cry for their husbands. They cannot find any work. They suffer," Zapeta told me. "When their men disappear, the women can't go back. They leave behind their houses, clothes, their communal life. Indian people want to hold close to their families. They miss their villages. But they cannot go back."

Within this grim context, the perseverance of indigenous peoples in resisting and fighting back is a sign of the continued strength of indigenous cultures. Despite the systematic repression and violence, hundreds of indigenous organizations, ranging from widows, refugees, and campesino unions to entire communities, have spoken out in defense of their rights. Daily, indigenous men and women continue to risk their lives to defend their people.

One such Indian woman is Rigoberta Menchú. Born into poverty in a small Guatemalan village, she worked with her parents, tending corn and beans on their small plot. At times they worked as day laborers on coffee and sugar plantations. When she was eight, Rigoberta started earning money for the family by picking coffee—thirty-five pounds a day for twenty centavos.

Rigoberta's father, Vicente, was one of the first in their region to seek justice and a better life for the Indian people. He began organizing an agrarian union, encouraging peasants to work together to receive a better return on their labor. The community was behind him, but the government, suspicious of his growing popularity, arrested and threatened to assassinate him. When he was eventually released, Vicente had to live in hiding to continue his activist work.

Many landowners paid Indians barely enough to keep them alive. Conditions were both difficult and dangerous. One day when Rigoberta was eight, the plantation owner sprayed the coffee fields with pesticide. Rigoberta's two-year-old brother, who was already suffering from malnutrition, was exposed to the fumes and died.

"The important thing is that what has happened to me has happened to many other people, too," said Rigoberta, who wrote about her family in her 1983 autobiography, *I, Rigoberta Menchú.* "My story is the story of all poor Guatemalans. My personal experience is the reality of a whole people."

Rigoberta remembers the day in September 1979 when her sixteen-year-old brother, who had begun organizing like their father, was seized by the security police. "They cut the skin off his head and pulled it down on either side and cut off the fleshy part of his face," wrote Rigoberta. "But they took care not to damage the arteries or veins so that he would survive the tortures and not die." On the seventeenth day of torture, Rigoberta's brother died. The following year, her father joined other peasant activists in a protest at the Spanish embassy in Guatemala City. Police stormed the building; it caught fire. Her father burned to death.

A few weeks later, soldiers captured Rigoberta's mother. The town's high-ranking army officials raped her repeatedly, and on the third day of her torture they cut off her ears. They were trying to force her to reveal where Rigoberta and her brothers and sisters were hiding. "She defended every one of us until the end," recalled Rigoberta. "Disfigured and starving, my mother began to lose consciousness. . . . They gave her food. Then they started raping her again. . . . Since all my mother's wounds were open, there were worms in all of them. She was still alive. My mother died in terrible agony."

Rather than destroying her, these atrocities strengthened Rigoberta Menchú's resolve to win freedom for her people. She became an activist and worked underground. "Instead of having freedom," she says, "we have experienced more poverty, more fear, and as indigenous peoples we have been enslaved. This can no longer continue, We must put a stop to it and continue struggling to recognize our own culture. We must struggle to regain our ancient identity."

Eventually Rigoberta had to live in exile, and wherever she traveled she spoke of the oppression of her people. She urged the United States and other wealthy countries to stop meddling in poor countries, to halt the flow of military aid. "We as peasants want tools," she said. "We don't want more war. We want clinics and schools. We want education for our children."

In 1992, Menchú became a controversial nominee for the Nobel Peace Prize. The Guatemalan government objected to her nomination because, as the foreign minister said coolly, she was linked to "groups that have damaged Guatemala's reputation outside the country."

In October 1992, on the five hundredth anniversary of Columbus's arrival in the Americas, it was announced that Rigoberta Menchú was the new Nobel Peace laureate. Seventy thousand people marched in the streets with her. "I only wish my parents could have been present," said Rigoberta. "As the end of the twentieth century approaches, we hope that our continent will be pluralistic. The only thing I wish for is freedom for Indians wherever they are."

With the $800,000 Nobel Prize, Rigoberta Menchú established The Vicente Menchú Foundation in her father's name to defend the rights of indigenous peoples.

❖

"We must remember who we are. But our people are afraid to speak out," Adrian Esquino Lisco of El Salvador told me firmly. He stood before me, barely five feet tall, dressed in jeans and boots, a straw cowboy hat on his head. Officially, El Salvador has no Indians, but at least 45 percent of its people have Indian blood; Lisco was chief of their National Association of Indigenous Salvadorans. "With massacres like this," he said, "many of our people won't even acknowledge that they are Indians."

On February 22, 1983, soldiers of the El Salvador army had driven into the village of Los Hojas, twelve kilometers from Lisco's house. Ranchers wanted the land used by the Indians for growing beans, corn, and other vegetables. To get rid of the native farmers, the ranchers brought in a death squad. When the shooting was over, seventy-four Indian men, women, and children were dead. Lisco knew them all.

"I had to denounce the killing of these seventy-four people at whatever cost," said Lisco. "Soon the death squads came after me. I had to hide in the fields. Eventually, friends helped me leave the country. I went to the United States and talked to U.S. congressmen about the repression of Indians in El Salvador. For a while, things got better, but there have been more killings in San Julian, Juayua, and other villages."

Lisco spoke out against these massacres, which were the work of the Salvadoran army. But as the editors of *El Salvador: Central America in the New Cold War* point out, "The Salvadoran army is not altogether an independent entity: it is equipped and trained by the U.S. government. . . . The United States may someday have to admit

Rigoberta Menchú, 1992 Nobel Prize laureate.

that its hands are stained with the blood of Salvadoran citizens."

Ronald Reagan justified U.S. intervention in El Salvador in order to "stabilize" the region and halt the spread of communism. "What we see in El Salvador is an attempt to destabilize the entire region and eventually move chaos and anarchy toward the American border," he once said while president. "Will we stop the spread of communism in this hemisphere or not?"

As in Guatemala and Nicaragua, the "stabilization" of El Salvador fell heavily on the indigenous peoples. It was in 1989 that the death squads announced they were going to kill Adrian Lisco. Indian friends in the United States sent him tickets to leave the country with his son. They hurried to the airport and checked their luggage. As they stood in line to board, an official stopped them.

"What is wrong?" Lisco asked. "What have we done?"

"Sorry," the official said, "we have orders not to let you out of the country. I know you are a good man. I won't arrest you, but I can't let you on the plane."

Again, Lisco called on Indian friends in the United States. They called Amnesty International, which pressured the U.S. State Department. A week later, the U.S. embassy in El Salvador said that it would help protect Lisco. His name stayed on the wanted list, but the army left him alone.

"If not for the help of others, I'd be dead by now," Lisco told me matter-of-factly. "But I am alive and will continue denouncing the killing of Indians and the denial of their human rights. Our people are still considered backward and uncivilized. Accused of being drunken thieves, they are thrown in jail or killed."

"What's the most important thing for people in developed countries like the United States to know about your people?" I asked.

Lisco was silent for a moment. He gazed off into the distance, then turned and looked into my eyes. "I hope people will try to understand how we feel," he said. "Since the arrival of the Spaniards in 1492, people like the Maya, Nahuat, and Lenca in El Salvador have lived in a permanent state of conflict. We have been at war with those who have tried to erase all our cultural patterns. It is a matter of deep grief.

"I would like Americans and Europeans to understand that Indian people desperately want to survive as Indians. I ask that they support our struggles, our initiatives. Support our spirituality. The main thing is to understand that so-called development is dangerous. If things are not done in harmony with nature, it is the wrong path. People begin thinking only about dollars. That's why we have catastrophes."

"What can we do about it?" I asked. "What can others do?"

"We need to listen to the elders, to the spiritual leaders. They can help us recover. To have a vision of how to live, we need to contact our own roots, in our own country. This is important for non-Indians as well. If you approach Indian elders in a proper way, you can learn many things that will be helpful."

I asked him to describe the proper way.

"Go with an open heart, with an open mind," Lisco replied. "Wherever you live, you can go to Indian people to listen, to see if there is something you can learn. If people in the West would look at us differently, they might realize how indigenous peoples have developed cultures that are rooted in their land. Indian cultures can serve as models for living on the earth. It starts with a spiritual sense of life—with giving thanks to nature and deeply acknowledging that we are creatures of nature. We must remember who we are, where we came from, and where we are going. We are part of nature—all of us."

❖

"Do you believe in magic?" asked Miguel Soto, a tall Costa Rican Indian, whose piercing eyes looked at me mischievously.

"*We* believe in magic," he said, not waiting for me to answer. "The principle of magic is to try. No matter how hopeless our lives appear to be, if we try we take the first step on the path to solving our problems, that's magic. That's the magic my grandmother taught me. She was the last of the Boto people. There are a few of us left who carry some of the blood, but she was the last real Boto. She left me this magic."

By the time Soto turned twenty, he had finished training as an agricultural specialist. Rather than start a professional career, he decided to help other Indian people without charging money. For ten years, he traveled among different tribes in Costa Rica, Panama, and Colombia, offering assistance and asking only food and shelter for his efforts.

"These people you worked with, do they feel endangered?" I asked.

"Yes, many Indian people in Central America are endangered. They need help and they know it," he said. "But remember, most people in the Western world are also lost. They have lost their connection with nature, which is essential. How will *they* be rescued?"

A girl of Mayan ancestry, Guatemala.

ANDES

PEOPLE OF THE MOUNTAINS

When I was thirteen, I was beginning to hate my mother," says Amaru, a twenty-eight-year-old Quechua man from the small mountain village of Ayacucho in the heart of the old Inca empire. "I was hating her because I was hating my roots. To be an Indian in Peru can be really awful."

In recent years, Amaru and I have had lots of opportunities to talk candidly, for on his many visits to the United States I have become something of a surrogate father to him. "If you look Indian," he told me on one such visit, "people taunt you, treat you like an animal. Teachers tell you, 'Bring me some alcohol, bring me your sister.' You don't know if you want to be an Indian at all. Sometimes you act like you are white and sometimes you act like yourself." Far more devastating than their taking of the Inca's gold, says Amaru, "is the way the descendants of the conquistadors are still taking the souls of our people."

"Nowadays, I don't think even one-quarter of the Quechua in Peru feel proud of being Indian," Amaru said. "I really don't see any happiness in my people. I see sadness in their eyes. They feel bad for being born Indian. I had to struggle very hard to be proud of who I am. The turning point came when I began to know my father better. Since I was a little boy, I knew that my father was a shaman, a medicine man. This was just a normal thing for me. I didn't give any importance to it. But when I was sixteen, I began to see that he was really extraordinary. I saw his skill in curing people, and I learned that all of his knowledge came from our ancestors. He began to teach me all his healings and introduce me to the world of natural medicine. This was the time when I woke up, the first time I could begin to feel proud about myself and my culture. For me, this was like being reborn. I was able to sing in the streets."

These days, however, the streets of Ayacucho and most other Peruvian towns are unsafe for visitors and residents alike. The entire country has been terrorized by a prolonged civil war. One night, Amaru told me, some of his friends were celebrating

A young Andean woman, Peru.

the marriage of their daughter. Suddenly a policeman appeared. "Let me have some beer," he demanded.

"We don't know you," they said.

"I want to drink," said the policeman. Clearly he had been drinking.

"Please leave," someone said. The policeman drew his gun and tried to kill everyone there.

"When they kill everyone, it's like it never happened," says Amaru. "Families disappear. Whole villages disappear. Then a month or two later, someone finds a hole containing hundreds of bodies. Sometimes they line people up by a canyon to make it easier—once the people are shot they fall into the canyon and the soldiers, or terrorists, or drug dealers, or whoever killed them don't have to lose time covering the bodies. It's a nightmare of blood, just blood and blood and blood. Nobody knows why."

And few want to ask questions. "If you see something, you'd better keep your mouth shut or they will kill you," says Amaru. "Soldiers come into our village and rape teenage girls. But who is going to say anything? These men are the law— you see? The law is raping girls. To me, Peru is now a land without laws. And I think our culture is going extinct, that the end is coming and it's going to be very hard. We have already lost so much of our knowledge. In fifty years there may be nothing left of us but paintings and photographs of how we were."

As part of his personal commitment to saving Quechua culture, Amaru began reviving the music of his people, playing the flute, repairing old instruments, listening to tapes, learning from the oldest musicians. He went to the temple

A Quechua mother and child in Peru.

ruins where the Incas had once played their music. And he went to their places in the jungle, up in the mountains—to hidden ruins, caves, and waterfalls. "I discovered that this music is not for listening," he said. "It is deeper than that. It touches your spirit, like the wind or the ocean. The Inca melodies come to me and make me cry. They make me feel alive and help me talk with God. They make me understand the happiness and sadness of the world. They help me remember that I am a part of nature, a part of the sunrise and rain in the jungle."

On a personal level, Amaru began to realize that he was using the music as a buffer from the violent realities of modern Peru. "My music is like a wall that shields me from the things people want to do to me and my people," he once told me. "Sometimes terrorists come and kill our animals to feed themselves. Then the police come and say that we work with the terrorists, so they take us to jail."

Amaru makes a modest living by selling pottery and playing music, but his calling in life is as a medicine man. He is one of the very few young Quechuas who know the old ways of healing. "My work is to see into the hearts of people," he says. "It doesn't matter to me what color, what race they are, I can see into them."

I once asked Amaru what he would like to ask of people outside Peru. I thought he would ask us to put pressure on the government of Peru, but he said, "I think I'd ask other peoples of the world to respect their ancestors. When you know your ancestors, you respect yourself. But we've lost our ancestors and have become enemies of ourselves. That is why we are killing ourselves."

✤

From one end of the Andes to the other, indigenous peoples have had to cope with the same forces of alienation, repression, and terrorism that Amaru described. The Quechua, Aymara, Mocovi, and dozens of other peoples speak—cautiously—of their governments' systematic attempts to destroy their cultures.

"All attempts to Europeanize or Americanize us are doomed to fail," said a coalition of Quechua and Aymara Indians in Bolivia. "We want economic development, but based on our own values. We do not want to lose the virtues we have inherited from our ancestors. We fear the development concepts from abroad because they do not consider our deepest values. These powers have never understood or respected the great treasures that the Indian soul possesses."

From Argentina comes another version of the same story. "The Mocovi people have been at war with Argentina since the beginning of the century," says Ariel Araujo, a young Mocovi man whose angelic face masks a fierce determination. "For many years Argentina boasted to the world that no indigenous people existed in its territory. It is only since we have been making international appearances that we are starting to 'exist' again."

I spoke, too, with a Mapuche man from Tierra del Fuego at the southern tip of Chile. When you shake hands with Chino Bustos, you can't help noticing that the ends of his fingers are gnarled and misshapen. When he was a teenager, the authorities suspected him of subversive activities and pulled out his fingernails. Now, living in exile in the United States, he thinks back. "I knew from the time I was eight years old and packing potatoes with my grandfather that the survival of my people would be my battle. My mother, my father, and all my family are fighters. Once we were all in jail at the same time and saw each other through the bars. I tried to stop the army from taking the lands of our village. And now I face a life sentence if I return to Chile."

An Aymara man from Bolivia shared his grief over living in exile from his people. "It is so hard to understand why everyone is against us. Many times we don't know how many people are left in a tribe or if they are gone altogether."

"My brother was held in prison and tortured for many months," Reynaldo Mariqueo, a Mapuche man, told me. "They arrested me, but couldn't prove I was a dangerous person, so they let me go. As soon as I was free, I ran away."

The stories go on and on—they are numberless and numbingly similar. Like thousands of other Chileans, Reynaldo Mariqueo has sought asylum abroad. He settled in England, found work as a printer and a graphic designer, and now has a wife and young child. "It was only after traveling to Europe," he says, "that I realized how much the Chilean government discriminates against the Mapuche."

The Mapuche have a long history of resisting adversity. They held off the Incas long before the Europeans came. When the conquistadors arrived, the Mapuche defended their homeland so fiercely that they won a rare concession from the Spanish—a treaty. In 1641, the Treaty of Quillan secured for the Mapuche twenty-five million acres, a third of their original homeland. For the next two centuries, they held intruders at bay, but in the 1880s the well-armed independent state of Chile defeated them, and the Mapuche culture has been under seige ever since.

By 1929, the original Mapuche homeland had been reduced to a million and a half acres divided among 3,078 widely scattered reserves. Between 1943 and 1947, legislative gerrymandering sold off vast tracts of the remaining lands without Mapuche consent. Then, in 1970, Salvador Allende won the presidency and began reversing decades of systematic abuse. Within three years, he had returned two hundred thousand acres of land to the Indians and created a special office of indigenous affairs. But in September 1973, General Augusto Pinochet staged a U.S.-supported coup, bringing an abrupt end to Allende's reforms. Mapuche who had supported Allende were routinely imprisoned, tortured, and executed by the police and paramilitary death squads.

As with so many indigenous cultures, the heart of Mapuche life is the community and its day-to-day relationship with the land. "But in 1979," Mariqueo told me, "they passed a law meant to destroy us by destroying our communities." Pinochet's law 2568 called for the liquidation of Indian communities and mandated that, if just one person in a community asked for title to a piece of land, the community had to divide its land. By 1985, this law had cut the number of Mapuche communities from 2,066 to 655. Their lands had been reduced to less than nine hundred thousand acres, about 1 percent of their original territory.

"At this moment in our history," said Mariqueo, when I met him in the summer of 1992, "the Mapuche are fighting very hard for salvation. We are determined to regain the lands that have been illegally taken from us. The government that has replaced Pinochet is trying to present a democratic image to the world and show concern for the rights of indigenous people. But in practice, they do very little. For example, the government says that Mapuche territory confiscated by the state and then sold to individuals cannot be returned to Mapuche. The law always favors the landowner over the Mapuche."

And yet the culture lives on. About half of the one million Mapuche now live in cities, where Spanish is the dominant language. But in the villages, most Mapuche children still speak their native language. "We Mapuche are very strong in preserving our identity and culture," says Mariqueo. "Some religious ceremonies almost disappeared, but they are coming back now. The old people are teaching the youngsters to dance, to sing, to conduct the traditional ceremonies. We are living in an era in which our identity is being revived. It's really amazing to be a part of it."

Of all the goals the Mapuche seek, the most fundamental is formal recognition by the Chilean constitution as a separate and distinct people. As long as Chile fails to recognize the Mapuche as an indigenous people, Mapuche human rights are not protected under international law. Says Mariqueo, "We are asking the government to revise the constitution to recognize the existence of the Mapuche, but our main goal is the adoption of a universal declaration of the rights of indigenous people."

❖

Throughout North America today, people wear the ethnic clothing of the mountain people from South America, admiring the warmth of Andean wool garments.

Creating a universal Declaration of Indigenous Rights has become a major objective of indigenous leaders everywhere. Many of us in the West, particularly in the more prosperous countries, may wonder why such a document is necessary. After all, when the United Nations was formed in 1945, it made a universal human rights declaration. However, while the United Nations gave meticulous attention to the rights of states and of individuals within states, it said nothing at all about the rights of indigenous peoples outside the mainstream to retain their separate ways. In the face of the continuing attempts of many governments to eradicate indigenous peoples, the United Nations's blanket guarantee has been revealed as empty sentiment.

"What governments have banked on in the past," writes David Maybury-Lewis, founder of the organization called Cultural Survival, "was the idea that if you stamped on all the specific manifestations of ethnicity, somehow you could prevent that potential from flowering into a full-blown sense of ethnicity. I think this is a hopeless task."

Julian Burger, of the U.N. Center for Human Rights, calculates that in half of the one hundred and sixty-one states in the United Nations, the rights of indigenous peoples to self-determination are being denied or restricted.

By various estimates, there are between two hundred and two hundred and fifty million indigenous people in the world, but dispersed as they are, they have little influence in the affairs of their countries and no official voice at all in the United Nations. And yet their very status as outcasts and their fierce desire to exist unify them in

A Peruvian Indian carries grass for her donkey.

ways unappreciated by the world's larger powers. In recent years, their leaders have begun to come together to gain the voice denied them in the international community.

This quest for representation at the United Nations has been a long and sometimes maddening journey through endless layers of protocol. For more than eight years, Reynaldo Mariqueo has scraped together the means to travel to Geneva to plead for indigenous rights. Rigoberta Menchú and dozens of other indigenous leaders have sacrificed their personal lives in pursuit of a Declaration of Indigenous Rights. Such a document, they believe, is essential for the survival of their people in the next century. Whatever form the final declaration takes, they generally agree it must guarantee that

▸ all indigenous populations have the right to self-determination, the right to chart their own economic, social, religious, and cultural destinies;

▸ all nations recognize their indigenous peoples and the rights of those peoples to their traditional lands and institutions;

▸ all indigenous peoples be afforded basic human rights;

▸ all indigenous peoples be allowed an education grounded in their own language and values;

▸ all indigenous peoples retain the rights to their artifacts, burial grounds, sacred sites, designs, music, art, and oral histories;

▸ all treaties made by indigenous nations be honored through national and international law.

If the United Nations fails to create and ratify a Declaration of Indigenous Rights, the Mapuche of Chile, numbering a million people with an unflinching determination to survive, may be able to struggle through the next century. Smaller and more vulnerable cultures are not likely to last.

❖

"It shall soon be the end of us, and therefore I want to tell you the last part," says a Tesere Guarasug'we tribesman. "There by the River Pauserna, we had lived in happiness. But today our end has come."

When this man's father was a young boy, white settlers came to their region for the first time and set out axes, knives, iron machetes, dresses made of cloth, and combs. "What joy when they saw all these things. Now my kinfolks had iron tools, but they were also lost."

When the villagers came to get the mysterious gifts, the whites surrounded them, shooting at those who tried to escape. Most of the villagers who survived this ambush were marched to Santa Cruz de la Sierra to be sold. "The whites raped the women and the young girls still virgins," said the remaining tribesman. "Almost all of the young boys and girls died on the way to Santa Cruz."

The Indians who had escaped into the hills were soon infected with diseases they had never known. "Many of us died of the fever. People simply fell dead while fetching water, talking with friends. My mother's sister got up one morning, set out for water and never came back. Relatives found the poor woman near the waterhole. Blood came out of her mouth. She had fever and they could hardly hear her last words: 'We shall all die if we don't get away soon.'"

But as one tribe after another has discovered, there are no longer places for escape. "You can see for yourself," said the Guarasug'we tribesman in 1977, "how small our tribe is now, and that our end is near." Sixteen years later, in the Year of the Indigenous Peoples of the World, barely a trace of his people has survived.

An Indian woman in Ecuador begins a grass basket.

AMAZONIA

PEOPLE OF THE RAIN FOREST

*C*ivilization must advance," read an 1854 report to the U.S. Congress on the Amazon's potential, "though it tread on the neck of the savage, or even trample him out of existence."

To explorers, missionaries, and all sorts of fortune seekers, the vast reaches of the Amazon have long beckoned as a last frontier waiting to be civilized. But for the people of the rain forest, the Amazon is simply their home. In the quiet light under the forest canopy, the rhythms of day-to-day life still play out much as they have for thousands of years. Over centuries of trial and error, these people have evolved ways of growing vegetables, hunting and fishing, and gathering wild fruits and nuts that allow the forest to replenish itself.

In recent years, images of the Amazon going up in smoke have jarred us into realizing that the rain forest is finite and fast disappearing. Fifteen percent of the Amazon is already deforested and an estimated twenty million acres of virgin forest are cleared annually. But what of the people?

Since the turn of the century, indigenous cultures in Brazil have been disappearing at the rate of one per year. As many times as I've read or reiterated this fact, I don't believe I've begun to fully comprehend the suffering it represents. It might be reassuring if we could relegate this enormous loss in the human family to travesties of the past. But we can't. If anything, the pace of cultural extinction in the Amazon may be quickening, as new roads are pushed through indigenous territories, bringing new waves of miners, settlers, alcohol, and disease.

A Jivaro father and son on the Momon River, a Peruvian tributary of the Amazon. Until 1982, their people shrunk the heads of their enemies.

"The indigenous societies in these tropical regions are becoming extinct at an even faster rate than the regions they have traditionally inhabited," says Jason Clay of Cultural Survival. "In many indigenous societies undergoing rapid change, young people no longer learn the methods by which their ancestors maintained fragile regions. Little time remains to salvage this knowledge."

Most of the Amazon's Indian societies are already extinct, and those that remain face imminent destruction. But is the extinction of these indigenous peoples inevitable? Brazilian law actually provides the assurance that native communities receive "permanent possession of the land they inhabit, recognizing their right to exclusive use of the natural wealth." However, another statute gives the government the right to expropriate Indian lands and relocate entire communities in the interests of national security or development. To provide the kind of security that allowed them to survive and evolve over millennia, native lands must be demarcated and then those boundaries rigorously guarded. Brazilian governments will, of course, come and go, some with less corruption and more commitment to indigenous peoples than others.

If they begin to accept, really accept that indigenous peoples are part of the environment, conservationists could play a pivotal role in the future of Amazon cultures. Each year, millions of dollars are spent to save endangered birds, mammals, insects, and snakes, but as yet there is only a minimal awareness that people can be endangered, too. Anthropologists, scientists, and grass roots activists everywhere could also greatly enhance the prospects for the survival of these people. But over the long haul, I expect the difference between cultural extinction and cultural survival in the Amazon is going to rest with the indigenous peoples themselves, who are just beginning to assert their rights. It was only in the 1970s that chiefs of various tribes began meeting each other. In 1980, Brazilian Indian leaders formed the Union of Indian Nations to address their common problems.

In 1992, several hundred Indian leaders gathered for a week near Rio de Janeiro to draft the Kari-Oca declaration of their needs and rights. I was priviledged to be there, amidst several hundred Kayapo, Xingu, Terena, Potiguara, Yanomami, and other tribal peoples from the Amazon Basin. Though they have their differences and lack many resources, there is a new generation of indigenous leaders emerging to tackle the problems that are likely to plague their people well into the next century.

❖

"We indigenous people from Brazil are totally different from the American and Canadian Indians, the Aborigines, and Maoris," said Jorge Terena. Sitting across from me with his great mane of dark hair hanging down over shoulders, he looked as if he could have just come from the jungle or another time. But he spoke to me in the perfect English that he had learned while studying in the United States for eight years—he became the first Brazilian Indian to earn a masters degree. "These other indigenous peoples," he said, "are a lot more developed than the Brazilians. In other countries, you find native people who are businessmen, lawyers, teachers, or other professionals, but not in Brazil. In other parts of the world, indigenous peoples already have access to the best technology their countries offer. We don't. Others have well-established rights, but here we still face the basic problem of having our people and organizations recognized by the government."

In many ways, modern Brazil is a stepchild of its turbulent past. Since the first European forays in the sixteenth century, as many as six million indigenous Brazilians have been killed or have died from European diseases. Nobody knows exactly how many Indians perished in the conquering of Brazil, nor even how many separate cultures have vanished. That is history, but the attitudes toward Indians formed in those times still shape Brazilian relations with its two hundred and twenty-five thousand Indians, which today account for for less than one-tenth of 1 percent of Brazil's population.

"Now that we are getting organized, they seem to view us as a threat, as if they don't want to lose control," says Terena. "We have to get

A Shimaco Indian loading bananas to be transported down the Amazon by boat.

A Majoruna woman of the Yavari River adorns herself with "whiskers" to emulate the jaguar for protection. She has eight children and refuses to send them to school, where only Spanish is spoken.

away from this, become independent. It's true that many tribes still depend on government officials to speak for them, but we want to break away from this kind of relationship. We can be our own spokesmen. We don't need anybody else to speak for us. We know how to speak. We know how to put our problems on the table."

One of the issues that Terena is raising at every opportunity is the question of intellectual property rights. "This is a new subject for us as indigenous people," he says. "We don't have too many people familiar with scientific jargon. But even if we don't know the meaning of words like *biotechnology* and *biodiversity,* we know what they are in practice. All the time we see people come to our village and take advantage of us. A scientist

will go to a village and talk to the elderly to learn everything they know about herbs and natural medicines. They take this knowledge and samples of the plants back to their laboratories. They apply for a patent, and then they own it. They sell the knowledge that came from the indigenous people. What do we get? Nothing.

"I think every country should have a law recognizing these intellectual property rights. But I am afraid that once again we are going to be left out."

❖

It is difficult to meet Eliane Potiguara and not notice her commitment to the struggle of indigenous women. As president of Grumin, an organization of five hundred indigenous women, Eliane directs a number of initiatives. Pottery is made to enable communities to earn at least a small amount of money. One education program offers training for Indian teachers, another prepares classroom materials based on indigenous realities. She also runs a campaign to curb alcoholism. "All of our men drink," she says. "They feel impotent because they have no prospects for work and they see their communities dying."

Eliane's own Potiguara people (a person's last name is often the name of his or her tribe) still number about seven thousand. In the past twenty years, they have suffered one setback after another. They always had enough land for their needs until the government parceled half of it out to develop sugar-cane plantations. Freshwater shrimp was once a staple in their diet, but now miners have polluted the river and it is unsafe to eat the shrimp. "Whether they mean to or not, all the people coming to our region play a part in destroying the way we live," Eliane told me. "We have lost our land. There is no work for the men. Babies are dying from lack of food. People feel helpless. We are caught in the chains of hunger, misery, drinking, violence, and suicide."

Eliane's own perseverance is sustained by

a deep well of spirituality. Any number of stories might illustrate her grit and determination, but I think the best way to get a sense of this remarkable woman is through her own words. Eliane wrote a poem in memory of her close friend Marcal Tupa, a Guarani chief who was assassinated in 1983. She speaks of it as her Prayer for the Liberation of Indigenous Peoples:

Stop pruning my leaves
And taking away my hoe.
Enough of drowning my beliefs
And chopping up my roots.
Have done with suffocating my mind.
No more of killing my chants
And silencing my voice.
The roots do not dry of those whose seeds
Are scattered on the ground to sprout.
Grandparents' gifts are not dimmed—
Rich memory,
Ancestral blood: rituals of remembrance . . .
Do away with the envy
And ingratitude of the powerful.
Give us light, faith, and life
In the sacred rites.
Lead us, oh Tupa, from violence and killing.
In a sacred place by the stream
On the nights of the full moon,
Oh Marcal, call
The spirits of the rocks to dance the Tore.
In the festivals of manioc and shamans
Bring us vital resistance . . .
Pray for us, bird of the heavens,

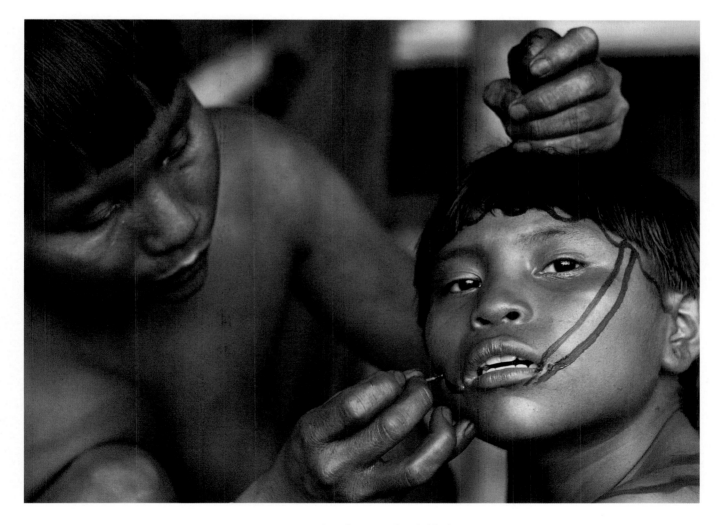

A Yanomami mother paints her child's face.

So that jaguars, wild pigs, toucans,
And capybaras
Come and circle the Jurena
And Parana rivers,
Because we are pacific,
In spite of everything . . .
Pray for us, shaman bird, every morning,
In the Amazon, in the arid lands,
And in the heart of a woman.
Make the children happy
Who are reborn of Indian bellies.
Give us hope each day
Because we only ask for land and peace
For our poor—these rich children.

❖

"There are many different ways to under-stand and to measure development," says Evaristo Nugkuag, president of COICA, the coordinating organization for indigenous groups of the Amazon Basin.

"We indigenous peoples have long had many different development models imposed on us and our territories by both the State and the private sector, and we have suffered enormously. If you want to know what development means to us, you must be willing to accept that our mode of development is not the same as yours. Our development is not based on accumulation of material goods, nor on the greatest rates of profit, obtained at the expense of our territories and future generations. . . . For us, development must take into account the future of an entire people."

The key to development from this in-digenous perspective is having an extensive and diversified territory where all people, animals, trees, and rivers will share the benefits. "We were taught by missionaries and development workers to raise cattle," says Evaristo. "But we are begin-ning to realize that we made a poor deal: We sac-rificed thousands of useful and potentially useful species just to feed a cow."

"There is no need to overly romanticize

Davi Kopenawa Yanomami. "We have two struggles: the fight to defend our land and our territory, and the fight to defend the earth, the trees, the sky, and the wind."

indigenous cultivators," cautions Jason Clay. "Some have been known to forget where they have planted seeds and needlessly replant the same area." But as Clay emphasizes, peoples of the rain forest are adept at "reading the environ-ment," and their land-use methods "are based on the view that the environment is the source of life for future generations and should therefore not be pillaged for short-term gain and long-term loss."

There can be no life if our forests are de-stroyed, says Evaristo. "We want to continue liv-ing in our homeland. We have no interest in tak-ing everything the forest has to offer and moving to the city to live in material comfort from the profits of our plunder."

Every year, half a million acres of forest go up in smoke in the Peruvian Amazon alone. To the Peruvian government this spells progress. To the Indians it is, in Evaristo's words, "a disas-ter that is impoverishing our people. To this day, hundreds of families are kept as slaves on farms or sent to cut timber, with no pay, no food, but

By the time they are ten years old, Yanomami boys develop enough skill with a bow to hunt birds and monkeys.

with armed guards. Young girls are kept captive in the landlord's house to service him at his will. Both young and old are mutilated and beaten for trying to escape. Tuberculosis is rampant. The local authorities know this is going on, but they close their eyes.

"Slavery still exists—right here at the end of the twentieth century. We live in crushing poverty. The authorities have a total disdain for our rights. Our forest has become a land of violence. Poverty, corruption, injustice, and lack of basic human rights all generate violence. And that is why the Amazon is so violent today."

❖

Prior to the 1970s, the Yanomami dwelled beyond the reach of the twentieth century in a remote area of northern Brazil and southern Venezuela. There were about twenty thousand Yanomami then, all living in small community groups that moved every four or five years to give the forest and their garden soils time to regenerate.

In 1973, the world of the Yanomami changed abruptly with the construction of Brazil's Perimetral Norte Highway, which cut through two hundred kilometers of their territory. The road workers introduced contagious diseases and prostitution. By 1975, four Yanomami villages on the Ajarani River had lost 22 percent of their people. By 1978, four villages on the Catrimani River had lost 50 percent of their people. In one Yanomami community in the Serra de Surucucus, 68 percent of the Yanomami died virtually overnight.

A second wave of death began gathering with the discovery of gold on Yanomami lands.

In August 1987, thousands of *garimpeiros,* the go-for-broke prospectors and roustabouts that chase every real or imagined mother lode, were pouring into the area from every corner of Brazil. By the next spring, the miners had built more than eighty illegal airstrips. During the first half of 1989, fifty thousand miners had invaded Yanomami territory. "In a matter of months," noted a report to the Brazilian government by Alcida Ramos, "major rivers became unusable. Mercury pollution [from refining gold] and silting drastically affected the entire course of the Macajaí River; poisoned with mercury and oil, the Uraricoera, Catrimani, and Couto de Magalhaes rivers stopped yielding fish. . . . In the first nine months of 1990, more than fifteen hundred Yanomami died, mostly from diseases, but many had been shot."

"When I was young, we weren't suffering like this," Davi Kopenawa Yanomami told me in Rio de Janiero in the spring of 1992. "When I was a boy, life was good. We weren't dying like we are today. Since the white people have come to our country, they have let us live in hunger, they let us suffer. I am talking like this so you can feel it inside your heart."

As one of the very few Yanomami who speak Portuguese, Davi has often been the sole emissary between his people and the outside world. When we've seen each other in Rio, Kari-Oca, and later at the United Nations in New York, he's always been very warm and direct. And every time we've sat together to talk, I've had the feeling of being in the presence of a person from another time and place. This sensation must arise in part because he comes from a place in the forest I will probably never see and from a childhood thousands of years removed from my own. But the pain in his voice is familiar, for he is right now living through the Great Death that Harold Napoleon's Yup'ik people endured a hundred years ago.

"The Yanomami are sick. We are dying," Davi said. "We don't know how to take care of the disease the gold miners brought to our land. It is the government's fault. It didn't think about us when it allowed the gold seekers to come in. We want to ask the world to help us pressure the Brazilian government into taking care of the indigenous peoples all over Brazil. We are asking them to send us doctors to exterminate this disease. I don't want my people to die."

For many years Claudia Andujar of São Paulo, Brazil, has worked with Davi and other Yanomami to protect their lands. "All the people who have studied the Yanomami and know them have different visions of the Yanomami," she once said. "I see them as intellectuals, as people who think about and understand the world in a global way. It is a vision as old as humanity, but we have lost it."

From my brief but memorable encounters with Davi Yanomami, I tend to share Andujar's view. "I need the help of your people to cure this sickness," Davi told me. "But concerning nature, I need to help your people. The Americans, the English, the Japanese—we want to teach their children and grandchildren not to destroy the earth anymore. The situation isn't dangerous just for the Yanomamis but for eveyone. We all live on the same planet."

And then, looking straight into my face, he said, as if he were talking both to me very personally and to my people, "I'm with you in this fight. I am not going to run away. But I am not going to be quiet. Whenever you need me, I'll help you, because the Yanomami need to fight in order that our brothers will not suffer.

"We don't have jobs and money. And we don't want these things from other cultures. Indians like us live in another world. And we want to remain Indians." Davi paused to make sure I understood. "The mountains, the rain, the wind, the moon, the stars, the sun—we need these to keep living. We want to remain in our culture, in our way of thinking. I want to be in my forest, listening to the birds, the thunders—breathing the pure air."

This Yagua man, living on a tributary of the Amazon in northeastern Peru, still uses a blowgun to catch fish and wild boar. Eighty percent of the Yagua are believed to be caught up in bonded labor; settlers and drug dealers often receive young Yagua girls as payment for debts.

AFRICA

TUAREG

THE BLUE PEOPLE OF THE SAHARA

An hour after sunrise, the cool night air has warmed. By noon it will be more than 110 degrees Fahrenheit. On a windy day, the sound of sand blowing across a thousand miles of desert is almost deafening. But this morning there is no wind, and the stillness is broken only by the sounds of a Tuareg camp coming to life. Barefoot children run in and out of the tents. Women dressed in blue muslin robes talk quietly as they sit cross-legged on the sand, heating a kettle of mint tea. Now and then, a goat bleats in the distance.

"With ten goats, five sheep, a couple of cattle, and a camel, a nomadic herder can make a life in the desert," Acherif Ag Mohammed tells me in French. He is a Tuareg in his mid-forties. His dark eyes are surrounded by deep creases from peering across the desert out of his protective blue-black wrap. "The Sahara is very livable," he says. "It's the only place where I feel at home."

"You don't need the modern world?" I ask.

"Yes, we need help from the modern world, but not at any price. I will share my anguish with you. I would rather die than give up our way of life. We must be free to travel the desert. But now Niger and Mali won't let us cross their borders."

"And if you try?" I ask.

Mohammed shakes his head and then looks into my eyes. "They shoot us," he says calmly. "They shoot our camels, goats, and sheep. They shoot our men. And when they can't get our men, they kill our women and children. In the past six months more than eight hundred innocent people have died."

For a moment I am silent, searching for words to honor his solemn disclosure. "You must get terribly discouraged."

"No. *Before* we felt discouraged. We knew despair. But the time for sorrow is over, finished. Now we are fighting for our lives. Soldiers stop us at the new borders, but to survive we need to move over a very large territory. We're nomadic because our environment is nomadic. The rain comes and goes. Every year the rain brings

*A Tuareg mother
and child, Mali.*

*Previous page:
A Maasai family,
Maasai Mara,
Kenya.*

fresh grass to a different part of the desert. We have to follow the weather. Traveling the Sahara is our life. It's who we are. If we are held back, our life is ripped from us. Every day we are becoming more like a people that is dying. But we will find a way to survive."

The Tuareg are survivors. For centuries they have endured the stark realities of the Sahara, persevering through windstorms, drought, starvation, and fierce desert battles. Today, however, their continued existence is threatened as never before. New nation-states are hemming in the Tuareg. The process of desertification is accelerating across North Africa. And in the future, their way of life as nomads and people of the caravans may simply have no place. Their challenge as a people is first to survive physically and then to redefine who they are and how they will live in the modern world.

Thurston Clarke, who lived among the Tuareg in the 1920s, wrote, "For many Tuareg, their first exodus from their homelands was indeed 'a last caravan,' and they died or remain scattered throughout the cities and sedentary regions of West Africa. They continue to live on charity or on their earnings as guards or laborers. . . . In a few decades they will become a weak and distorted echo of an earlier generation."

In a sense, the Tuareg of today are refugees from another era. Their forebears were also refugees, believed to be descendants of the Berbers, a Caucasian people, who were early inhabitants of North Africa. When Arab armies advanced onto their lands, some retreated into the Atlas Mountains of Morocco. Others sought to preserve their tribal ways by heading into the desert. These desert dwellers called themselves Kel Tamashek, "the people who speak Tamashek." The Arab invaders called them Tuareg, "the abandoned of God."

The Tuareg became nomads of the open desert. Until the beginning of the twentieth century, they reigned over the caravans crossing the Sahara. Some were traders. Others sold their services as guards to Bedouin and Arab caravans plying cloth, spices, gold, and slaves to and from tropical Africa. If their offer of protection was rejected, they were apt to raid the caravan themselves. Either way, the Tuareg developed the skills and bearing of great warriors.

When the French began colonizing West Africa in the late 1800s, they found the Tuareg formidable. One Frenchman who saw the blue-veiled men charging on their camels said, "The shrill cries of the warriors, the sound of the javelins flashing through the air, and the long lugubrious beat of the tobol drums. . . . To see a Tuareg war charge is to feel complete and utter fear creep through one's body."

The French and Tuareg waged bloody battles, guns against swords, in the desert outposts of Hoggar, Tit, and Timbuctou. "If we wish to stay in this desert country, we must try to pacify it without pity for the Tuareg," reported one French officer. "The Tuareg does not have any more reason to exist than the American Indian, but unhappily the climate of the desert and their fantastic camels have put obstacles in our way that were unknown to the Americans. It is nevertheless possible to overcome these obstacles."

By 1920, French artillery had subdued the Tuareg's curved sabers and great courage. However, under French rule, the Tuareg could still move about the Sahara much as they pleased. And with open hostilities ended, they enjoyed a period of relative stability and prosperity. But the era of their great caravans was coming to an end, and with it part of the soul of their culture.

"We were all the time trading salt, cheese, dates, butter, and smoked meats with other caravans," recalls Acherif Ag Mohammed. "But the need to barter is disappearing. Goods are now shipped by trans-Sahara lorries or by boat. Every year we have fewer caravans, fewer camels. And the biggest problem is that our caravans are now illegal."

An indigenous woman, Burkina Faso.
Modern Africa is the product of European colonialism,
which took millions—some believe as many as one hundred
million—of indigenous Africans in the slave trade and
then physically occupied the continent.

In 1960, Tuareg caravans and their no-madic freedom in the desert faced an unexpected impasse. When the French pulled out of North Africa, the vast open reaches of the Sahara were divided into new independent states of Algeria, Libya, Mali, Burkina Faso, and Niger. While the end of colonial rule brought a new sense of free-dom for some North Africans, the nomadic Tu-areg found themselves boxed in by new bound-aries and hostile military regimes. Colonial rule had kept traditional animosities at bay; now they were let loose. The new nation-states zealously guarded their new borders. Overnight, the Tuareg lost the freedom to move across the land, which is the very essence of being Tuareg.

"The years of independence since 1960 have been a nightmare for us," says a friend of Mohammed, who, fearing for his safety, speaks anonymously. "During this period we have known only military administration, the law of the gun, contempt, injustice, and hatred. Mali obtained the support of Algeria and Morocco in a common anti-Tuareg front. We faced daily summary and public executions, our camps were razed, our water holes mined and poisoned, and our herds machine-gunned. France remained silent. No one tried to stop the massacres or even to renounce the genocide of a people who were struggling for survival."

From time to time, Mali or Niger would declare a truce, and some of the Tuareg refugees would return to their homelands. In December 1989, for example, Tuareg chiefs were given the assurance that their people could live peacefully in Niger. About twenty thousand Tuareg returned. But soon tensions increased. Tuareg were arrest-ed for no apparent reason. When their friends and families protested, fights broke out. Less than six months after the truce was announced, a gov-ernment official announced that "all the Tuareg must be counted and exterminated."

Mali reoccupied the oases where the Tuareg came nearly every day in search of water for their animals. "The soldiers wait there and shoot at anyone who approaches," said one survi-vor of an attack. "Some groups have been totally destroyed. They've been beaten to death, cut to pieces, and hung. They've been burned alive and buried alive. There have been public rapes."

About one million Tuareg have thus far survived the cycle of truces and massacres that come and go with the whims of the short-lived North African regimes. However, even were a permanent truce achieved, the future of the Tuareg would be far from secure. As another man, who asked to remain anonymous, said, "We no longer have the right to speak our own language, and our children are forced to learn the language of others. Our traditions are ridiculed. Our youth are encouraged to become wayward. And our daughters are at the mercy of Malian soldiers—many are mothers and facing a life of poverty before they reach fifteen years of age.

"But we have a culture, a history, a language, a writing system—and we used to have a country. Must we disappear in order to impress upon the world the scandalous injustice we are suffering? Are we wrong to want to continue living according to our own customs and culture? Is it a crime to live a nomadic life?"

Even if political constraints were removed, the nomadic way of eking out a living from the Sahara and the arid *sahel* would be marginal at best. Most Tuareg prefer to live as nomadic pastoralists—breeding camels, cattle, goats, and sheep. But closed in by private lands and national borders, they have nowhere to lead their animals in times of drought. During the three-year drought

A nomadic mother and child, Ethiopia.

in the early 1970s, an estimated 125,000 Tuareg slowly starved to death.

"Tranquility exists in the shade of sabers," goes a Tuareg saying, which served them well for centuries of strife in the desert. Today, however, the Tuareg also need to adapt to the realities and combat the politics of desertification. In the past, to a traditional Tuareg herdsman it was suicidal to destroy a living tree, an indispensable source of shade, food, shelter, fuel, and tanning materials. But today ever more trees are being cut to be burned and made into charcoal, which is then sold to save one's animals and family from starvation. As trees disappear, fewer roots grip the parched ground. Wind scatters the thin soil. Sand dunes advance. The policies of governments and multinational corporations disregard the tough but vulnerable desert ecology.

Today, the Tuareg must face enemies within themselves as well—their own despair, feelings of hopelessness, and acts of desperation. As desertification advances and competition for scarce resources increases, age-old patterns of respect for the land slip away.

Recently, a friend traveled the Sahara by camel with several Tuareg herdsmen. For three weeks they crossed a stretch of desert without seeing a single bush or tree. Then one morning they came upon a solitary tree rising from the sand. Judging by its size, it must have been at least a hundred years old; its lower branches had long ago been grazed back to stubs by goats and camels. A herdsman dismounted, climbed the tree, and began picking leaves for his camel. He picked until there was not a single leaf left.

An Oromo woman, Ethiopia. Although in the majority, the Oromo are not allowed to speak their language in schools and other public places. Amharic people, representing only 15 percent of the population, dominate the country's government and its eight tribal peoples.

MAASAI AND BUSHMEN

"WE CAN ONLY BE HUMAN TOGETHER"

*L*ong ago, so the treasured story goes, an ancient people was barely surviving in an arid land surrounded by steep, unclimbable cliffs. The rains failed. Cattle were starving, and so were the people. But there was one sign of hope: The people saw flying birds with green grass in their beaks. The elders sent out scouts to follow them, and these seekers eventually found a perilous route over the mountainous rock walls to a land of lush and fertile pastures. Together, the people built a bridge and began climbing out of the valley of death. As they were crossing over with their cattle and sheep, the bridge suddenly snapped, hurling many back into the barren valley. The fallen people became known as the *Ilmeek*, the "others." Those who succeeded in reaching the new world were the Maasai.

Tall, stately, and renowned for their warrior heritage, the Maasai make their home on the open plains of the Great Rift Valley in East Africa. Numbering about half a million, they now dwell in settlements called *kraals* scattered throughout "Maasailand," which crosses the borders of present-day Kenya and Tanzania.

"I hope your cattle are well," one Maasai will often say to another when they meet, for among the Serengeti's vast herds of wildebeest, antelope, and zebra, it is cattle that play the central role in the lives of these majestically tall, slender people. A family's wealth is measured by the size of its herd, daily life is governed by the need for fresh pasturelands and water, and guarding the cattle from thieves and wild animals is the main work of the men. As a test of their ability to meet this responsibility, young men are sent out alone, armed only with a spear, to kill a lion.

But today there are greater tests than lions challenging the strength of the Maasai. Armed with no more than their courage and cultural values, the Maasai, along with myriad other tribal peoples throughout Africa, struggle to sustain a meaningful way of life in the wreckage left by colonialism.

In the 1800s, with no regard for the ecological and cultural viability they found there, Europeans carved up Africa into a hodgepodge of forty-eight

A Maasai woman, Kenya.

possessions. The borders they imposed cut through the homelands of indigenous ethnic groups, parceling off the fragments among the new colonial states. Disregarding native concerns, the British and Germans splintered Maasailand into three fragments—Tanganyika, Kenya, and Uganda—and ignored or attacked ancient tribal institutions as primitive and beneath their interest. Not until the 1960s, when many African states won independence from the colonial interlopers, did the restoration of native rights become a possibility. But no sooner did the colonial governors move out of their mansions than African leaders, obsessed with their own new power, moved in. Far from honoring the ancestral claims that enriched the cultural diversity of the continent, with new vigor these new rulers reasserted the colonial boundaries.

Writes Moringe Parkipuny, executive secretary of a grass roots organization of pastoral peoples in Tanzania, "The essential task of nation-state building has in consequence suffered across the continent and fallen into a quagmire of boundary disputes and endless wars."

The result has been not the hoped-for restoration of ancient tribal lands, but rather a fanning of competition for diminishing resources. Today, Maasai compete with other tribes and—ironically—with national game parks for the use of the semiarid savanna where they have lived for centuries as nomadic pastoralists. Although the Maasai way of life hinges solely on access to grazing lands, most Maasai now have less than half the land they need to sustain their herds. The result is overgrazing, which renders unseasonable dry periods disastrous. One drought in the early 1960s took a third of all Maasai cattle.

It is true that the tourist industry has found a way to protect a remnant of East Africa's irreplaceable animal resources—exclusion of the Maasai from their traditional homelands. So one resource is showcased while a proud and dignified people is thrown into crisis. In places, tourist fees have been shared with resident pastoralists, but money has never been an adequate substitute for an indigenous way of life. Without their land and cattle, the Maasai will soon cease to exist.

❖

"I grew up here, unconscious of the beauty of the landscape but aware of the abundance of the wildlife," recalls Maasai writer Tepilit Ole Saitoti. "When I was young, I would chase zebras with my friends until we were swallowed by the dust and had to shout so the zebras wouldn't trample us as they stampeded by.

"I never confronted my father except when we talked of why he chose me of all his children to go to school. . . . 'Why me?' I would ask. School to the Maasai was a bad thing, a place where children were taught alien ideas incompatible with Maasai values, a place where people were indoctrinated and got lost."

Trekking with his father, Tepilit asked him, "Did I cry that first day when you sent me to school?"

"You cried blood tears," said his father. "You were choked up all day and you made the whole village weep."

"Did I cry each time I went back to school after holidays?"

His father replied that even though he had cried every time he returned to school, his family was depending on him to learn how to communicate with the outside world. Still, he cautioned his son, "You must be careful, because being away in any place for a long time could lead you to forget our ways. Try to learn the new ways while retaining our culture. God was not a fool to make us Maasai."

After a long silence, Tepilit's father went on, perhaps talking to himself as much as to his son. "How can I tell you to travel on a path that I have not traveled? I would rather tell my children to follow in my footsteps and be able to alert them to all the obstacles along the way. I would be able

A Namibian elder. Sixty-two thousand San Bushmen live in Namibia, Botswana, and Angola, but only about three hundred still live a traditional nomadic life.

A Maasai elder, Kenya. "The Maasai are in distress; they are crying out for help," writes Tepilit Ole Saitoti of his people. "But we are still holding on and continue to celebrate our culture despite the urgent demands that we change our ways."

to tell you to keep the river on the right or the left and to cross it at a certain point. The new happenings are strange and frightening, like all unfamiliar things. In your youth's mind, you have crossed over to the other bank, but I advise you to stop, wait for a while and observe before proceeding ahead. . . . [Then] perhaps you will help us to cross a bridge—a weak bridge over a frightening flood. . . ."

"My people are still holding on and continue to celebrate our culture despite the urgent demands that we change our ways to assimilate to contemporary modes of living," writes Tepilit. "If change must come, as seems inevitable, it must be gradual, not abrupt. My people are in distress; they are crying out for help. They are determined to live. The Maasai will live. We will adapt. We will survive."

❖

In the film *The Gods Must Be Crazy*, a dark-skinned Bushman, slight of stature and nearly naked, runs across the dry African grassland. He stops suddenly. Lying before him on the ground is an object of great mystery—an empty Coke bottle. Never having seen one before, he assumes it has fallen from the sky, and he sets off to return it to the gods. Millions of moviegoers around the world, including myself, were charmed by the delightful innocence of this man, who lived in an idyllic world far beyond the turmoil of the twentieth century. Unfortunately, the film created a completely distorted impression of the Bushmen, much to their detriment.

"Far from being 'beautiful people living in primeval paradise,' they are in reality the most victimized and brutalized people in the bloody history that is southern Africa," writes Robert Gordon, an anthropologist who grew up in Namibia, in *The Bushman Myth*. "If we anthropologists are concerned about the future of humanity, then it is incumbent upon us to try to understand the processes by which Bushmen were brutalized. More important, we need to understand why no scientists seriously addressed the issue of why Bushmen were becoming 'extinct.'"

Before the arrival of Europeans, the San and !Kung people, who would become known as Bushmen, lived a nomadic life, sharing their few possessions and moving with the seasons from one camp to another. Their paintings of wild animals on desert rocks indicate that they were living on the plains of southern Africa at least ten thousand years ago. They survived by hunting and gathering wild nuts, roots, and fruits. With an abundance of wild game, they had time to make music, dance, and tell stories. Their world was the whole of southern Africa and, in many respects, it *was* the natural paradise that many of us, from afar, imagine Africa to be. Vast herds of springbok, wildebeest, zebra, giraffe, and elephant moved across the savanna, and the Bushmen moved with them.

"Ever since there have been Bushmen in the world," says one, "we have never killed one of these great animals without saying thank you to it with a dance for allowing itself to be killed so that we could live."

With some twenty-five thousand Bushmen in Botswana, twenty-nine thousand in Namibia, and eight thousand in Angola, these people are not in immediate danger of disappearing as a racial group. But they are as close to cultural extinction as any indigenous people. The encroachment of cattle ranchers in Botswana and the internecine warfare in Namibia have made it all but impossible for the Bushmen to continue their nomadic way of life. Squeezed into a desolate corner of the Kalahari Desert, at most several hundred Bushmen still live the life of their ancestors.

The collapse of Bushman culture began when the first Europeans arrived in the mid-1700s. It suited these strangers' purposes to see the Bushmen not as charming innocents but as lazy and wretched heathens. The Germans and Dutch who settled in South Africa sanctioned the killing of Bushmen and the taking of the women as concubines. They justified this posture with the assumption that, after all, it was only a matter of time before the lowly Bushmen disappeared from the face of the earth.

"What can the civilized human being manage to do with people who stand at the level of [the Bushmen]?" wrote geographer Siegfried Passarge in 1907. "Jail and the correction house would be a reward. . . . Does any possibility exist other than shooting them?"

Between 1911 and 1912, the Germans launched more than four hundred armed patrols to search Bushmen areas and break up their settlements. Officers were ordered to shoot "in the *slightest* case of insubordination against officials," or when a suspect "being hunted down *does not stop on command* but tries to escape." Since Bushmen were known to flee at the sight of any patrol, such policies were in effect warrants for murder.

"The Bushman has always run away . . . and they have been killed off like predatory game," wrote the German anthropologist Leonard Schultz, who suggested "preserving the Bushmen in reservations as the last remnants of the primordial past of the human race."

Victimized as they were by the European invasion, it is not accurate to characterize all Bushmen as helpless victims. At first, they fought for their lands, but their bows were no match for the settlers' guns, and they died by the thousands. Then, as their culture disintegrated around them, they found new ways of surviving, sometimes ways that their forebears would have abhorred. "Instead of toppling helplessly from foraging to begging," writes Robert Gordon, "they emerge as hotshot traders in the mercantile world market for ivory and skins. They were brokers between competing forces and hired guns in the game business . . . they appear as one of many willing agents of this commercial depletion."

Willing agents of destruction? That is one way to look at it. But another way is to see the Bushmen's activities as desperate responses to the degradation of their culture and themselves as human beings. Not only did the coming of European immigrants greatly diminish the wild game in the Bushman's homelands, but it disrupted and degraded Bushman culture beyond description.

Only a few Bushmen now possess the necessary skills to live as hunter-gatherers. But more poignantly, most have turned their backs on the old ways in shame. Today's Bushmen are "a non-people," writes Laurens Van der Post, a scholar and Jungian psychologist who has worked and lived among the Bushmen for more than forty years. "They are a tattered remnant clinging to the edges of the industrialized world. . . . The most tragic thing about the Bushmen is the clear sense they have of their own inferior status. We have unremittingly taken away their land and their livelihood and are still doing so today.

We have failed to recognize that in their own context their values have as much validity as our own. We have also failed to recognize that until we came to southern Africa they had a way of life that worked. We did not. Now neither they nor we have a way of life that truly works."

Although the Bushmen, living as Bushmen, have all but vanished in our time, their culture still speaks to us, perhaps now more than ever. "When I sought to understand the primitive in ourselves," writes Van der Post, "the Bushman became a kind of frontier guide. . . . The essence of this being, I believe, was his sense of belonging: belonging to nature, the universe, life and his own humanity."

In times past, the Bushmen's sense of belonging encompassed every breathing, sighing, singing creature, every twig and leaf. The earth and sky and all that moved were family to them. They were at home in their world, as few modern people have ever been at home on the earth. Today we can peer into the heart of atoms and walk upon the moon, but somewhere along the way most of us have lost the sense of belonging, of being at home in a place on the earth and within ourselves. In time, we may look upon our footsteps in the lunar dust as tracks left by someone looking for, as Van der Post puts it, "this shining sense of belonging, of being known."

❖

The Bushmen are hardly the only native group in Africa torn apart by an intruder's blindness to their value. The anarchy that colonialism bequeathed to Somalia has turned Africa's Horn into a cornucopia of misery. The region encompassing Somalia, the Sudan, Kenya, Ethiopia, Eritrea, and Djibouti is mired in a vicious cycle of banditry, warfare, and famine that has left more than twenty-four million people in dire need of emergency food and medical supplies.

Nobel Laureate Bishop Desmond Tutu, with characteristic directness, reminds us that within the national borders of South Africa millions of native people "have been turned into aliens in the land of their birth . . . stable black communities have been destroyed and those who have been uprooted have been dumped as you would dump not people but things. . . . This cancer, eating away at the vitals of black family life, is deliberate government policy."

But the same clarity of vision that allows Bishop Tutu to see into this heart of darkness also illuminates for us all the simplicity of the healing solution, were we only capable of embracing it together: "Africans believe in something that is difficult to render in English," he writes. "We call it *ubuntu, botho*. It means the essence of being human. You know when it is there and when it is absent. It speaks about humaneness, gentleness, hospitality, putting yourself out on the behalf of others, being vulnerable. It recognizes that my humanity is bound up in yours, for we can only be human together."

A Himba mother and child in northern Namibia.

MALAGASY

THE VISE OF HUNGER

M adagascar is the naturalist's promised land," wrote the French explorer Philippe de Commerson in 1771. "Nature seems to have retreated there into a private sanctuary where . . . you meet bizarre and marvelous forms at every step."

Two centuries later, naturalist Gerald Durrell reports that "Madagascar, its plants, its animals, and its people, are in the gravest danger. It is essential that the rest of the world realize the biological importance of the island and the plight of its people, and hurry to rescue this extraordinary corner of the planet."

Madagascar has been called "a world out of time" and "the place time forgot." But in recent years, this island-continent in the Indian Ocean has become a metaphor for our troubled era, and perhaps the precursor of a future in which the politics of poverty and pressure of overpopulation extinguish both wildlife and people.

Like the Galápagos Islands, where Darwin shaped his theories of evolution, Madagascar's isolation rendered it a world unto itself. About 175 million years ago, the land mass that would become Madagascar separated from Africa and began drifting east. A thousand miles long and the size of France and Switzerland combined, it now lies off the east coast of Africa. Eighty percent of Madagascar's flora and fauna are found nowhere else on earth. Among its four hundred species of reptiles are half the world's chameleons—the smallest can perch on one's finger, and the largest is a blue-green giant, about a yard long, that preys on small birds. The island's evolutionary well has poured forth eight thousand species of plants, including a cactus that grows twenty feet high, towering hundred-foot baobab trees, and more varieties of orchids than grow anywhere else in the world.

Madagascar was the last of the large land masses to become inhabited. Its first people arrived in outrigger canoes from present-day Indonesia just fifteen hundred years ago. The seafaring pioneers must have possessed great self-reliance to load their families into canoes and set out on a four-thousand-mile journey

A Malagasy man beside his family home in Madagascar.

A Malagasy woman harvesting rice.

Madagascar was the last large land mass to become inhabited. About fifteen hundred years ago, its first people arrived in outrigger canoes from present-day Indonesia.

across the Indian Ocean with no charts or promise of land beyond the horizon. But for all their ocean-going skills, these people evidently did not bring with them the kind of respect for nature that characterizes most indigenous peoples.

Within a century of their arrival, Madagascar's first inhabitants had extinguished several extraordinary creatures. They used primitive spears to hunt the giant lemurs to extinction. Once found in many parts of Africa and North America, lemurs were displaced there by smarter and more aggressive monkeys. They are now found only on Madagascar, where thirty or so species—including the aye aye, a cat-sized lemur with ears like those of bats, and the tiny mouse lemur, at sixteen ounces the world's smallest primate—live on the steeper rain forest slopes, the drier desert regions, and hidden away in labyrinthine limestone crags of the Tsingy region.

The first Malagasy also hunted the great land tortoises and pygmy hippos to extinction.

And they gathered the unprotected eggs of the aepyornis, the fabled "elephant bird," until the last of these flightless birds had vanished. Other species disappeared as successive generations of Malagasy burned the forest to plant crops.

Once nearly covered with trees, Madagascar has lost four-fifths of its virgin forest to indiscriminate logging. Rains that once brought renewed life to the hills now eat away exposed topsoil, leaving the steeper slopes riddled with deep gullies. An astronaut circling the earth once remarked that "Madagascar seems to be bleeding to death." Satellite imagery has shown the Indian Ocean stained red fifty miles from shore with the island's lost soil.

"The Earth is the first wife of God; it cares for the living and embraces the dead," says a Malagasy proverb, which seems to suggest that humans are the recipients of the earth's bounty but are not necessarily an inseparable part of nature. Here, the world view of the Malagasy departs from those of most indigenous peoples and comes closer to the frontier thinking of the pioneers who settled nineteenth-century America. Wealthier Malagasy carved large tracts in the forest to make room for sugar, orange, and banana plantations. Year after year, they cut trees in the belief that there would always be virgin land, another forest to clear, more fields to plant.

Today, the Malagasy comprise numerous tribal groups, related to one another by a common language. Some of these tribes have more sustainable lifestyles than others. The elusive Mikea are hunter-gatherers who have no noticeable effect on the waterless western forests where they live in small bands. With survival skills reminiscent of Kalahari Bushmen, they dig for the *babo* roots that are their only source of water for months on end. Another group, the Vezo, are heirs to their ancestors' seafaring ways. Known as "people of the paddle," they fish the coastal waters, gather clams and urchins at low tide, and have little impact on the land.

However, the vast majority of Malagasy do take a toll on the land as they scratch out their meager living growing rice, maize, and manioc. They live on the fringes of the cash economy with an average income—combining both cash and the value of subsistence goods—of less than $250 U.S. a year. Many do not earn or grow enough to feed their families. Malnutrition is widespread.

"We have before us the specter of Ethiopia," says Remy Tiandrazana. As the people suffer, so does the land.

In the way of their Asian ancestors, Malagasy farmers used to let hillside rice fields lie fallow for ten to fifteen years, giving the soil time to regenerate. But driven by hunger and competition for planting sites, many of them now plant fields every five years. As a consequence, the soil becomes depleted, yields drop, and the farmers feel compelled to clear more forested areas. Once villagers have cleared land, they often burn it annually to stimulate the growth of new grass. Every year much of the countryside goes up in smoke.

People have been using fire to clear land for at least ten thousand years, and millions of tribal people in tropical and subtropical regions still use fire in their swidden, the so-called slash-and-burn, farming. Indiscriminate burning has drastically altered many landscapes, but done properly, slash-and-burn techniques have minimal impact. When indigenous people had access to extensive areas of arable land, they were able to sustain their slash-and-burn farming indefinitely by rotating their burning and planting from one hillside to another over the course of years. In many parts of the world, tribal people are still using fire to improve pasture for wild and domestic animals; to promote the growth of nuts, berries, and seeds; and to clear fields for planting. In Asia alone, some two hundred million people, many of them tribal, still practice slash-and-burn agriculture.

In northern Thailand, the Pwo Karen, who consider land sacred, take great care when burning a field to control their fires. Lua villagers in India rely on their priests to determine the best time to burn and then conduct ceremonies throughout the burning to satisfy spirits of the fields. In northeast India, the Garos people take care to appease the forest gods and then begin their cutting and burning with festivities, feasting, song, and dance. In Sarawak, Dyak village priests follow a carefully prescribed ritual for setting a trial fire. They choose an auspicious day, prepare a sacrificial meal, scatter the meal as an offering to the spirits, and then begin burning carefully selected plants from the clearing. If this sacrificial trial burns well, they know it is the right moment to prepare their fields for planting. All these people share a deeply held belief that their cultivation has a sacred dimension. The clearing, burning, and planting must all be done with great care.

In *Slash and Burn,* authors Peters and Neuenschwander assert that traditional slash-and-burn farming is ecologically sound because the fires are usually contained and the fallow periods sufficiently long. But they warn that the situation is rapidly changing: "The emergence of millions of non-traditional shifting cultivators is tipping the balance toward environmental degradation. Drastically increased population pressure is the nexus of the crisis."

In Madagascar, the slash-and-burn crisis is driven by a population that is increasing 3.1 percent each year. At this rate, the 1989 population of 11.25 million will triple by 2015. On the average, Malagasy women give birth to six children. Family planning programs have been started, but they are unlikely to slow the birth rate until the nation's education, health care, and standard of living can improve. Until then, children will represent security, working in the fields by the age of six and eventually caring for their aged parents.

Impoverished and lacking opportunities for employment, the vast majority of Malagasy men have no alternative but to eke out a living by farming. To coax more food from the land, they burn between one-fourth and one-third of their island's surface every year. The burns stimulate rapid regrowth of grass, providing pasture for their zebu, a variety of hump-backed cattle, at the end of the dry season. But over the long run, this annual burning encourages the growth of tougher, less palatable grasses that hold most of their nutrients in their roots.

Some of the fires the Malagasy set are intended to increase the runoff to rice paddies. The short-term gain is an early planting; the long-term loss can be measured in tons of soil. From year to year, the once life-sustaining rains erode deep gullies into the hillsides. Minerals and organic materials leach from the soil, leaving sun-baked laterite, in which only coarse bunch grass thrives.

Malagasy men. The average family income in Madagascar is less than $250 a year.

But each year, the combination of lower soil fertility and more mouths to feed forces farmers to clear land higher in the hills. A typical field of mountain rice on a forty-degree slope may lose up to five hundred tons of topsoil a year. As more soil is lost, the destructive cycle accelerates, and the vise of hunger tightens on both the Malagasy and the island's endangered species.

For decades, in its pursuit of export-oriented economic development, Madagascar neglected the environment. Financing from the World Bank and investments of multinational corporations spurred development projects. But Madagascar, like other countries that have tried to jump-start their economies, soon found itself saddled with a staggering national debt and depleted natural resources.

Because of their extreme poverty, the Malagasys' impact on their island's environment has been called "a tragedy without villains." Still, impoverished or not, Madagascar's people will end up bearing the responsibility and living with the consequences of that tragedy. From a distance, it is easy to suggest that they preserve the land's productivity for their children and grandchildren. But for those whose survival is a day-to-day struggle, the future is too far away to contemplate. The challenge in Madagascar, as in all Third World countries, is to connect the long-term needs of the people to a sustainable level of resource use.

The earliest conservation efforts in Madagascar failed because they were based on Western desires to preserve the island's exotic creatures, with little or no regard for the local people. Simply making it illegal to clear a forest had little effect. Landless peasants with hungry children were more concerned with where their next meal would come from than with the fate of a ring-tailed lemur. Knowing that the people had no practical alternatives, officials usually looked the other way when they caught someone clearing trees.

But by the mid-1980s, the government began to realize that the welfare of the people was inextricably linked with environmental protection. "Before, people only spoke of the beauty and scientific interest of our flora and fauna," says Joseph Randrianasolo, former Minister of Livestock, Water, and Forests. "This time we are speaking of our people *and* how to manage our resources to be self-sufficient in food and fuel wood."

In 1985, an improbable alliance of Madagascar officials, the World Bank, and conservation organizations began to set the country on a course of sustainable development. The World Wildlife Fund made an extensive survey of the island's forests. The government and World Bank then forged the survey's conclusions into the National Environmental Action Plan. With a fifteen-year scope, the plan spells out direct actions for preserving biodiversity, providing peasants with land tenure, curbing soil erosion, and initiating agroforestry. It also provides environmental education at the grass roots level—an essential step for linking social and ecological issues.

The effectiveness of Madagascar's Environmental Action Plan will depend on the commitment of those who carry it out. If lending agencies, conservationists, and government officials keep working with the local people, they have a chance of reversing the island's self-destructive course. In the end, salvaging Madagascar will rest on the realization of farmers and herdsmen that their future lies in restoring their island's ravaged landscape. Progress toward a sustainable future is likely to appear in small increments, as individual farmers cut back annual burning and start planting trees to restore their island's forests.

The Malagasy have a proverb for enduring friendship: *Rahanoriana no lany ny ala atsinana,* "It will have no end, like the eastern forest."

Malagasy men. The challenge in Madagascar is finding a way to connect the long-term needs of the Malagasy to a sustainable level of resource use.

EUROPE / ASIA

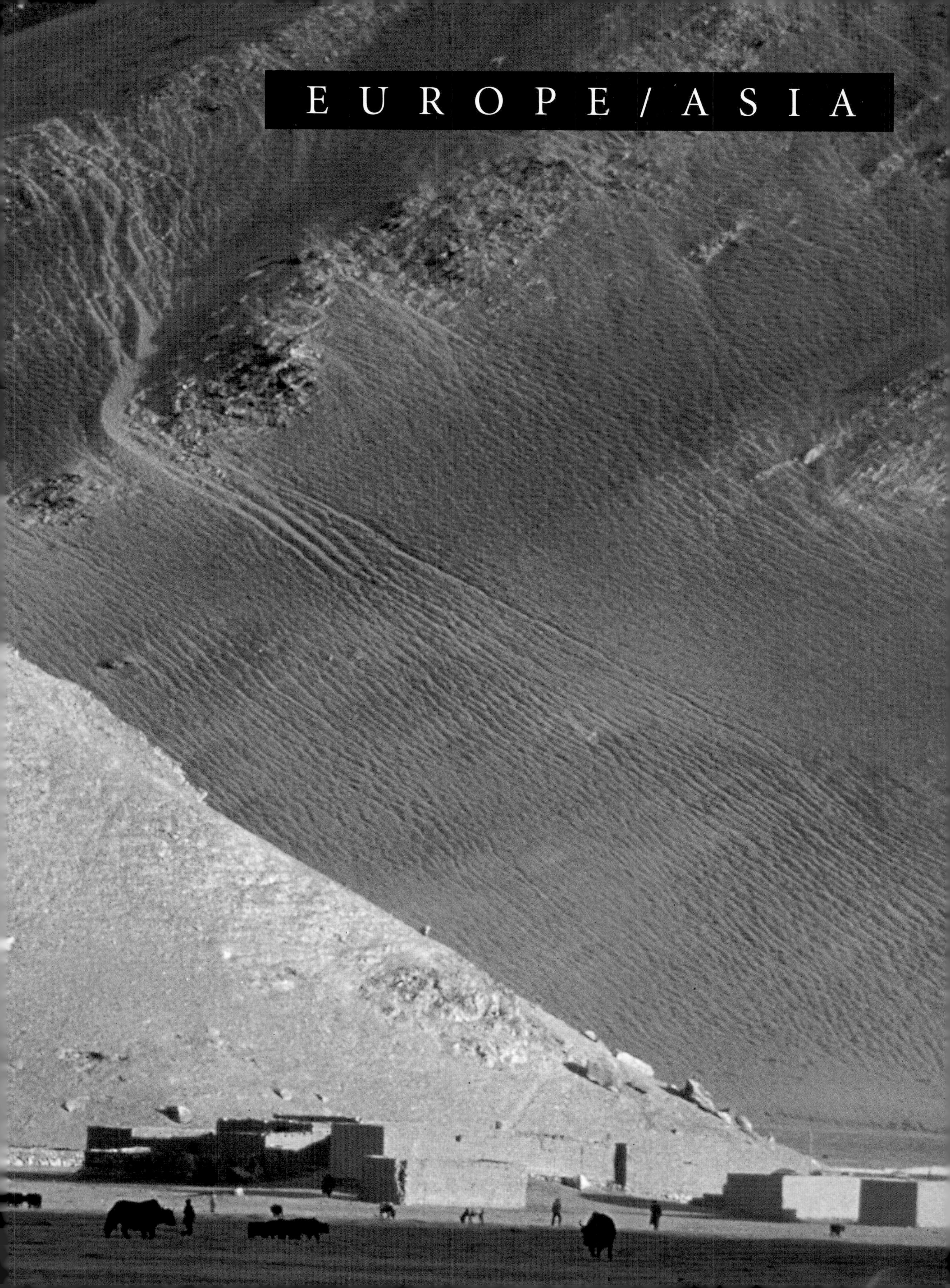

THE "SMALL PEOPLES" OF RUSSIA

"THE TIME OF ILLUSIONS IS OVER"

Natalya
Ivannikova, an
Even woman of
Magadan, Russia.

————

Previous page:
A Tibetan village
in the Himalayas.
More than half the
world's three
hundred million
indigenous people
live in Asia.

I can only be what I am. But when I was a little child, even a teenager, I was ashamed of being Sami," said Jill Aslaksin, a lovely young woman who spoke English, Norwegian, and Russian in addition to her native Sami. "I didn't dare speak our language in public or use our costumes."

In the spring of 1992, I visited Jill, who lived in Norway, and her Sami friend from Russia, Vladimir Afanoskier. The Sami people (often called Laplanders) native to the northern territories of Scandinavia and Russia, are Caucasian, with fair skin and hair. Like other indigenous peoples, they have their own songs, dances, myths, traditions, and distinctive ways of living from the land. In times past, most of them herded reindeer, moving freely across the windswept north. Now, their people and lands are split among Sweden, Norway, Finland, and western Russia, and their quality of life depends greatly on where they live.

"In Norway, we've tried hard to be heard and respected," Jill told me. "Over the past twenty years, our influence here has grown. And things are better now. I can be Sami without being ashamed. I live beside a good salmon river. I love to fish, and very often go to the mountains and forest to hunt and pick berries."

"You're very lucky," said Vladimir, at thirty a boyishly handsome man. "The difference between your life and ours in Russia is the difference between heaven and hell."

I asked him to elaborate.

"We have every problem you can imagine—getting jobs, food, a place to live. In Russia, my people are afraid to speak Sami in public. Most of our schools have been closed. We still have our traditional way of dressing, but now only the women have these clothes. Most men just don't have the money to buy cloth for shirts and jackets in the Sami style. Many, many Sami men in Russia have no jobs or land."

After a moment's reflection he went on. "If we had our land again, we could live without jobs." Before the Communists took over in 1917, Vladimir explained, many small Sami villages lined the coast and rivers. "My grandfather and uncle fished on the open sea. My mother fished for salmon in the rivers. Every fall, people moved their reindeer to a winter range, returning in the summer when the grass was high. But one day the Communists came and claimed our reindeer for the government. When they took the reindeer away, it was as if they took life right out of us. Since then, over the years, a lot of people have moved in from the villages to Louyardia, a kind of reservation. This place has no traditional houses, no separate plots of land, only a single big building with five floors. Earlier this year, a cousin of mine moved there. Sixteen people live in two rooms. Normal life is not possible. Most people have no possibility of working. They start drinking, and gradually, one by one, they kill themselves."

It was a grim statement of fact that by now I had heard many times in these interviews. I recognized the profound emotion in Vladimir's sudden silence and sensed what he was about to say when he continued.

"Many people, not just a few, have committed suicide. In my own family, two cousins and an uncle. Just before he killed himself, my uncle was drinking very much, because the struggle was too great for him. We struggle with everything—to find a place to live, to have enough to eat, to get from the government an area where we can herd reindeer. Everything is difficult. Very difficult. But if we just had our territory and traditional ways again, we could take care of ourselves."

I asked him how things had changed since the sudden dismantling of the Soviet Union. "Yes, the old government is destroyed, but the situation of the Sami people remains the same. Russia is more democratic, or attempts to make itself so, but to us it looks like the same old officials facing the same old problems. The Sami people are dying out, and we can't last much longer. In 1913, my village had about one hundred people. Now we have only forty-eight."

Again he was silent. Then in a flat voice,

he said, "And those of us who are left? I don't know. Seventy percent of the Sami men are not married. To have a wife and children, you need a house, a job, at least a little money for eating. Our men rarely have jobs or money. So the Sami women marry Russians. And for now," he said with a shrug and a sad smile, "it makes sense. A Russian perhaps has a good friend in the administration, someone who could help him get land to build a house. But for a Sami there are no more land rights. I had a family but I couldn't even get an apartment. Only for Soviet people, they told me. Could I bring my wife and daughter to live in my mother's one-room apartment?"

"What did you do?" I asked.

"We got divorced. My wife married a Russian. I visit my little girl on holidays—Russian holidays."

❖

At the other end of Russia, in the Soviet Far East, the Inuit of Chukotka, along the Bering Sea coast, live in a world different from that of the Alaskan Inuit. It was not the turbulent Bering Strait but the political gulf between the United States and Russia that split these people apart. When the Iron Curtain clanged shut after World War II, it became illegal for Inuit families to visit their relatives on the other side.

I was moved, on a hunting trip with some people from St. Lawrence Island, to look across the water and see the rolling hills of Siberia on the horizon. From where we were, we could have reached the Russian coast in an hour. Yet most Inuit, in their effort to reunite their people, have been unable to bridge this gap in their lifetimes. Still, there were bold attempts, even during the height of the Cold War, when jets regularly patrolled the skies. And sometimes there were unplanned encounters: Alaskan Eskimos who took their boats far out to sea or journeyed over the pack ice in winter might suddenly come upon some of their own people from Russia. Person

Tamara Khutkovaz wears traditional reindeer dress at a herders' camp on the Taigonosk Peninsula in the Russian Far East. She holds a willow-filled bear skull, kept to placate spirits.

to person, beyond governmental eyes, they would share a cup of tea, exchange news of their families and maybe a few personal items, and then return to their separate countries.

By the summer of 1992, tensions between the United States and Russia had relaxed enough for Ludmila Ainana, a leader of the Chukotka Inuits, to travel to Inuvik, Canada, to attend the Inuit Circumpolar Conference. Though it was a long journey to a place she had never been, for Ludmila the trip was like a homecoming.

"Inuits in Russia's north must learn your unity and perseverance," said Ludmila, a small woman in her fifties, to the Inuit from Alaska, Canada, and Greenland gathered at the conference. "In hard times, we recall your faces, your eyes, your thoughts, your ideas. Here we are together: We share one past, we can and must have one future. Real self-government, real democratic changes, are in the making in Russia. The [old] system kept people from determining their own destiny. That system is broken now, but its consequences will be felt in the future. We are still timid in taking power into our own hands."

In earlier times, there had been nothing timid about the Inuit of Chukotka. They had prospered in one of the world's most severe climates, where temperatures plummeted in the

Ketyi Ekaterina. Chukchi, Magadan region.

three months of total winter darkness to sixty degrees below zero. In the days of the czars they fiercely resisted all attempts to colonize them, but after the Russian Revolution, a wave of settlers moved into the region and simply overwhelmed them. Russian was taught in the schools. Newly created collective farms took over traditional hunting and fishing activities. The government ran fur farms and reindeer herds; it opened gold, tungsten, tin, and coal mines.

When Stalin's regime sentenced slave laborers to Siberia, it was to the cold and barren camps of Chukotka, the notorious gulags, that they came. The native people of the region were

shuffled around to accommodate them, as if they, too, were prisoners of the system. The Inuit village of Naukan, for example, was closed down in 1958. The people were relocated and lost everything they had—homes, land, means of livelihood, and the close ties with other people in their community.

"One of the most serious aftereffects of the Communist era," Ludmila told the gathered Inuits, "was that for many decades we were taught to submit to authorities, to rely on others, and to hope for the best. Now we must learn to survive in the competitive atmosphere of capitalism." Her people, she explained, also had to learn to address the despair expressed, with such numbing consistency, in alcoholism, suicide, and violence. "The average suicide and murder rate of indigenous peoples of Russia's north," she stated, "is three to four times higher than in the rest of the country. My kinsmen are becoming more and more impoverished and frustrated."

But Ludmila pushed past the note of despair to articulate firmly the only possible solution. "The government must transfer land rights to us," she said. "The core of the new policy toward us should be the formation of our own small nations, so that our lives can be anchored in our own ethnic traditions."

❖

This basic desire of people to anchor their lives in the traditions of their ancestors runs deep throughout the world. In places as diverse as South Africa and Bosnia-Herzegovina, it has spawned the tragic aberrations of apartheid and "ethnic cleansing." Among indigenous Russians, their need to live in the way of their people may also fall victim to a resurgence of ethnic hatred. But thus far it is flowering into a peaceful, if hard-fought, cultural revival. With the strictures of the government loosened, people are coming together, talking more freely, organizing, demanding their human rights and the return of their lands—in short, reasserting the initiative and resilience that enabled them to survive as distinct cultures for thousands of years. And once again they are acting on instincts that have lain fallow for eighty years.

"The time of illusions is over," said Chuner Taksami in March 1990. At a historic meeting in Moscow, he and leaders of twenty-five other indigenous peoples of the Soviet Far North met for the first time. "We all live in the severe northern climate, and we are all very few in numbers," said Taksami. "But there are also many differences between us. Each people, however small, is unique, and its disappearance would be an irreparable loss. The small peoples

of the North are confronted with the question of whether they shall continue to exist or forever disappear from the face of the earth."

Speaker followed speaker in demanding the constitutional changes that would secure their peoples' niches in whatever assemblage of states might emerge from the confusion of the new era. In the tug-of-war between the old guard and democratic reformers, central planners, and free-market advocates, the indigenous peoples simply want to remain themselves. More than anything, they ask for their birthright—their traditional lands. No issue is closer to their hearts or more vital to their future.

To some, the vast reaches of Russia's tundra and stunted taiga forest seem a harsh and empty land. But to the Nanets, Khants, Koryaks, Evenki, Yakuts, and other indigenous peoples of Russia, the land is the giver of life and all that is essential to it. There are salmon, whitefish, grayling, and trout in the rivers, and pike in the lakes. Along the coast, there are whales, seals, walrus, polar bears, sea otters, and many varieties of water fowl. Inland, the Chukotka landscape is much like that of northwest Alaska—vast expanses of tundra with dwarf willows, berry bushes, moss, sedges, lots of moose, caribou, wolves, bears, foxes, and many small fur-bearing animals.

These northern regions also contain the country's largest reserves of oil, gas, hard-rock minerals, and timber. In response to its runaway inflation and a desperate need for hard currency, Russia is pressing for the development of these natural resources.

"We have become hostages in the hands of the industrial ministries," says Taksami. "Ministries and local authorities are continually building new industrial enterprises, railways, nuclear power plants, and hydroelectric stations. They are making plans for the extraction of oil and gas from new fields and for felling enormous stretches of forests. As a consequence, the ecology and conditions for hunting, fishing, and reindeer herding are deteriorating rapidly. Living conditions have been damaged for all our peoples—without exception."

Jens Dahl, co-director of the Copenhagen-based International Working Group for Indigenous Affairs, reports that "the state development companies show no respect for the vulnerable arctic and subarctic ecology. If the industrial process continues unchanged, most of these indigenous cultures will disappear."

The Udegeh people of the Soviet Far East are an example. For more than seven hundred years, they have shared the Sikhotealin Mountains with Siberian tigers, whom they regard with a reverence that borders on worship. "The tiger and the Udegeh people are the same," goes a saying of the Udegeh, who would not think of harming one of the large cats. However, only eighty or so tigers and barely two thousand Udegeh people are left in the region, all threatened with extinction by the South Korean conglomerate Hyundai, which intends to log the hunting grounds they share.

When they heard that logging was to begin, six Udegeh hunters used a good part of their savings to charter a helicopter so they could fly to the hunting grounds and guard the trees with their rifles. Said one, "The logging will destroy our livelihood and culture." In response to their gesture, twelve Cossack soldiers from Vladivostok flew in to "defend the border." The trees were logged.

Farther west in Siberia, the development of one of the world's largest oil and gas reserves has already displaced many indigenous Khants. First these native people lost control of their lands, then oil field workers settled in the area. The Khants soon found themselves unemployed and shut out of the decision making.

"We should be in the red book of endangered species," said one Khant delegate to the 1990 Moscow meeting of the twenty-six groups. While all of Russia's indigenous peoples want their cultures to survive, many are struggling

for physical survival, period. "Life is too hard, and there's simply no time to think of something as abstract as culture," says Zaochynaya, a Kamchadal of Kamchatka. "We have to care for our daily bread first."

Among indigenous Russians, the incidence of tuberculosis is more than twice the national norm. In the past twenty years, life expectancy has dropped from sixty-one to forty-seven years, more than ten years below the national average. As native people have died and others have moved onto their lands, Russia's indigenous peoples have become stark minorities. By 1990, within the span of just two generations, in the regions that had been their tribal homelands since time immemorial, the Dogans, Chuckchi, Nanets, and Khants had all been reduced to less than ten percent of the resident populations.

Ironically, until the 1950s, Russia's indigenous peoples had been reasonably well protected. Many had received educational opportunities and priority hunting and fishing rights. They were well represented in party organizations and generally treated with respect and appreciation. But by the 1960s, a cultural meltdown had begun: Russia tried to break its indigenous cultures with aggressive policies of assimilation. The government made shamanism and many family rites illegal. It confiscated sacred objects. It set up boarding schools and enrolled native children, regardless of the wishes of their parents. And it destroyed villages hundreds of years old, moving the people and leaving the houses abandoned or bulldozed out of existence. Thousands of native people were forced from their lands to become workers at centralized farms and factories, while five-year plans hatched in Moscow brought thousands of immigrant workers into the indigenous regions. Most of the prime hunting and fishing areas were taken away from the indigenous populations and given to those who came north to make easy money.

"The government emphasized our backwardness," Taksami said of the workers and settlers who poured into the indigenous regions. "They ignored our culture and way of life. They looked upon anything ethnic as something to be exterminated. They rarely showed any care for the northern environment. They poached salmon from the rivers and shot wild animals at will. Money was their only incentive. Most didn't even try to understand the values of the indigenous peoples. From this treatment, we are losing the feeling of our worth and dignity."

Today, no more than 50 percent of Russia's Khant and Nanets people can speak their own languages. Unless a new course is set, most of their languages will be dead within another generation. "My children speak only Russian,"

says a native leader, who is fluent in Nanets and Khant as well as Russian. "There is little reason for them to speak the local language. Besides, we have no textbooks. Our culture is dying out."

As part of Russia's assimilation policy, indigenous languages have been almost completely excluded from the northern boarding school system. A whole generation of children has grown up without knowing their language or who they really are. "We all know very well that the boarding schools tear children away from their families and their culture," said Taksami. "This creates parasitical attitudes and a consumption mentality, which make young people unable to live our traditional way of life. . . . We are now standing at a turning point in our history."

Boris and Vargarita Tineru. Chukchi, Magadan region.

TIBET AND CHINA

A CULTURE IN EXILE

We wanted to be left alone," stated the Dalai Lama, political and spiritual leader of the Tibetan people. "It was a successful philosophy for one thousand years, but it failed us in the mid-twentieth century."

Tibet is a land that stirs the imagination: prayer flags fluttering in the cool thin air; monks, monasteries, and the towering rock ramparts of the Portola, home of the Dalai Lama; and the mountains, the highest in the world, their jagged white peaks soaring into the sky. Throughout history, Tibetans have cherished their world beyond the world, and for many centuries the Himalayan mountains have isolated Tibet, allowing its culture to flourish.

"We increased our natural isolation by allowing the fewest possible foreigners into our country," the Dalai Lama explained. "We had . . . no ambition whatever except to live in peace and pursue our own culture and religion. . . . For many Tibetans, material life was hard, but they were not victims of desire. We were happy. We admired simple living and individual responsibility. Among our mountains, there was more peace of mind than there is in most cities of the world."

In 1950, Tibet's isolation came to an abrupt end when the People's Republic of China declared Tibet to be part of itself and set about dismantling Tibetan culture. The invasion, along with the occupation and famine that followed, took the lives of one million two hundred thousand Tibetans. One million two hundred thousand? It is a number impossible to comprehend. How can we relate to such loss? The American people were traumatized when we lost fifty-one thousand of our young people in the Vietnam War; the Tibetans have lost more than twenty times as many people, many of them women and children. And Tibet is not a large country—before the invasion, its population numbered only six million. Its experience with China has taken the life of nearly one out of every five Tibetans.

Countless other Tibetans languish in prison. How many, no one knows—the Chinese have prohibited human rights organizations such as Amnesty International

An indigenous man in China, where the seventy million people of ethnic minorities constitute 7 percent of the total population.

• 115 •

A Tibetan woman sifting wheat. "All six million Tibetans should be on the list of endangered peoples,"
says the Dalai Lama. "This struggle is my first responsibility."

from entering the country. One man's letter was smuggled out of a Tibetan prison and eventually reached Cultural Survival. "Thieves and murderers are in the prison, too, but political prisoners are treated worst of all," the Tibetan prisoner wrote, not knowing who, if anyone, would read his words. "They don't want to kill political prisoners outright, as that would be scandalous in much of the world, but they treat us very badly. We can have visitors only once every three or four months, and then for only two minutes. And, of course, there is torture in prison.

"We are given only enough food to keep us from dying. We work breaking rocks, making paper, packing cement. We are not allowed to speak to one another. And we are given political instruction about how good the Chinese Communist Party is, so our [old] thoughts will be destroyed and we will be new people. Every month there is an execution meeting at which all the prisoners are gathered together to watch. Guns are loaded and the condemned person

is brought in. All the prisoners are gathered together and are told: 'You had better be good. You had better love the Communist Party. This person didn't. His life is forfeited.'"

On the night of March 17, 1959, the Dalai Lama escaped the threat of death himself by disguising himself as a laborer and fleeing his country. After a fourteen-day journey by foot through the rugged passes of the Himalayas, the Dalai Lama crossed the border into India, where he and those who accompanied him into exile were given sanctuary. To date, about one hundred and twenty thousand Tibetans live in exile, all but five thousand of them in India and the neighboring kingdoms of Nepal and Bhutan. In India, the exiles cluster together, and wherever they are, their communities tend to resemble Tibetan villages. A Buddhist temple, or a center for making traditional handicrafts, or a restaurant featuring Tibetan food—all these might spring up on foreign soil. But most important to the refugees, if it is at all possible, is the building of a school, where their children can learn Buddhist philosophy and the Tibetan language, the dual centers of the Tibetan culture.

In this way does the displaced culture thrive—in a freer form outside Tibet than within its trammeled borders. In a sense, the culture itself has become a refuge for an indigenous people shut out of its home. "Tibetan exiles are refugees, not as individuals but as a nation," says Tsering Wangyal, editor of the Delhi-based *Tibetan Review*. "The purpose of our escape from Tibet was not to save our lives, but to continue a distinct way of life. The secret of survival of Tibetan culture lies in the fact that it is a culture that we live every day in our ways of talking, behaving, and thinking. It is part of what we enjoy and what we abhor. It is, in short, what we are. And as long as we are determined and happy to be what we are, our culture remains alive."

China's annexation of Tibet is strikingly similar to Iraq's invasion of Kuwait. Both Tibet and Kuwait were the victims of totally unprovoked attacks. Both were targeted for their resources: Kuwait for its oil, Tibet for its timber, uranium, and other valuable minerals. On three separate occasions, the United Nations has passed resolutions demanding that China stop killing Tibetans and recognize their right to self-determination, but the Chinese government has failed to respond. Neither the United States nor any other nation has stepped forward to challenge China. In fact, in the very period during which China entrenched itself in Tibet, the United States granted China Most Favored Nation trading status, providing

A Wieger girl, China.

A Tibetan refugee. Since the Chinese invasion in 1950, roughly 20 percent of all Tibetans have been killed and hundreds of thousands forced into exile.

a variety of economic benefits and incentives to foster the exchange of goods.

China coupled its invasion with a systematic plan to eliminate Tibetan culture. One of its most insidious tactics has been the resettlement of Chinese within Tibetan borders, in a single generation rendering Tibetans a minority in their own country. Since 1949, when only a handful of Chinese families lived in Tibet, China has resettled seven million Chinese there. This massive influx has crushed the sustainable resources and lifestyles of the nomadic Tibetans, whose per capita income ($80 U.S. in 1990) and forty-year life expectancy are now the lowest in the world.

The Tibetans who have survived within Tibetan borders under Communist rule are engaged in a day-to-day struggle with a regime that seems determined to eradicate everything that makes them uniquely themselves. Monasteries have been destroyed. Schoolchildren are forced to learn Chinese—only Chinese—and a China-

biased version of history in school. The available jobs go to the Chinese. Some Tibetan women have been forced to marry Chinese men. Others have reportedly been sterilized. Thousands of young Tibetans have been sent to China. And all Tibetan dances, songs, and religious ceremonies have been prohibited.

As if these monolithic actions were not demoralizing enough, the Chinese also developed *thamzings,* a sort of revolutionary gauntlet designed to degrade the indigenous Tibetans. One regional Tibetan leader described the *thamzings* he had experienced as "diabolically cruel criticism meetings where children were made to accuse their parents of imaginary crimes; where farmers were made to denounce and beat up landlords; where pupils were made to degrade their teachers; where aged lamas were made to fornicate with whores in public; where every shred of dignity in a man was torn to pieces by his own people, his own children, and his own loved ones."

Throughout this program of cultural decimation, the Dalai Lama remains an inspiration to the refugees, with gentleness yet unswerving resolution reinforcing their belief in themselves and in their dream of returning to Tibet. In *Settlements of Hope,* Ann Forbes recalls how several thousand refugees in Nepal huddled together in the snow-covered fields under the shadow of the Himalaya Mountains to listen to a stranger read a message from the Dalai Lama. "Now we have come to the land of another people," he said. "Do not lose your heart. Do not be discouraged. Hope, hope is there. Wherever you are, keep good relations with the local people. We may face some problems with communication—but try your best. Be friendly with your neighbors and, most importantly, stay with the Tibetan community."

❖

In 1939, when the Dalai Lama was barely four years old, senior monks from the Lhasa monastery recognized him as the reincarnation

An old man with donkey cart, China.

of the Buddha of compassion. As a child, he was anointed His Holiness the Fourteenth Dalai Lama, spiritual and temporal leader of Tibet's six million people. Over the years, he has come to embody Tibetan culture and the struggle of Tibetans everywhere to regain their country. But even more than this, the Dalai Lama has come to represent the common struggle of all people everywhere to reclaim and affirm their humanity.

"My religion is simple. My religion is kindness," the Dalai Lama once said. "It is in our own interest to create a world of love, justice, and equality, for without a sense of universal responsibility based on morality, our existence and survival are at a perilous precipice. At present the world is suffering from great conflicts. . . . [The] solution is not technological or political, it is spiritual: a sensitive understanding of our common situation.

"Peace and survival of life on earth as we know it are threatened by human activities that lack a commitment to humanitarian values. Destruction of nature and natural resources results from ignorance, greed and lack of respect for the earth's living things. This lack of respect extends even to the earth's human descendants, the future generations who will inherit a vastly degraded planet if world peace does not become a reality and if destruction of the natural environment continues at the present rate."

Since the Chinese invasion, more than 40 percent of Tibet's forests have been cut, resulting in massive landslides and contributing to the extreme siltation of the Yangtse and Indus rivers. China's disposal of nuclear and other toxic wastes is contaminating parts of the Tibetan Plateau and already causing congenital deformities among nomadic herdspeople, livestock, and wildlife.

Before the Chinese invasion, Tibet had an abundance of wildlife, but by 1990, thirty Tibetan animal species—including the giant panda, snow leopard, and black-necked crane—were listed as endangered. Numerous reports have surfaced of the Chinese military using automatic weapons to wipe out entire herds of wild yak and wild ass.

"We have always considered our wild animals a symbol of freedom," says the Dalai Lama. "Nothing holds them back. They run free. So, you see, without them something is missing from even the most beautiful landscape. The land becomes empty, and only with the presence of wild living things can it gain full beauty. Nature and wild animals are complementary. People who live among wildlife without harming it are in harmony with the environment. Some of that harmony remains in Tibet, and because we had this in the past, we have some genuine hope for the future. If we make an attempt, we can have all this again."

To remain hopeful and determined in the face of seemingly insurmountable odds requires deep faith. "In my lifetime," the Dalai Lama has said, "I have seen a tremendous amount of suffering, a tremendous number of people killed by other people. It would be easy to have a pessimistic view of human values and truth, but trust and optimism are equally important. In our case, when we think of our experience of the last forty years, since the Chinese invasion, we remember that some of Tibet's closest friends very sadly and confidently expressed that Tibet was gone. There was no hope. Now we know that Tibet has not died. From the ashes and ruins it is slowly rising."

In the Dalai Lama's vision for the future, "Tibet need no longer be an occupied land, oppressed by force, unproductive and scarred by suffering. It can become a free haven where humanity and nature live in harmonious balance, a creative model for the resolution of tensions afflicting areas throughout the world."

In 1989, the Nobel Committee awarded the Nobel Peace Prize to the Dalai Lama, recog-

nizing him as the political and spiritual leader of the Tibetan people and praising his philosophy of peace, which is based on "reverence for all things living and upon the concept of universal responsibility embracing all mankind as well as nature." He embodies the struggle of endangered people everywhere and accepted the Nobel Peace Prize in a spirit of optimism, saying, "We must seek change through dialogue and trust. It is my heartfelt prayer that Tibet's plight may be resolved in such a manner and that once again my country, the Roof of the World, may serve as a sanctuary of peace and a resource of spiritual inspiration at the heart of Asia."

❖

In the spring of 1993, in the tiny office of the Tibetans Rights Campaign in Seattle, Washington, I had a chance to visit with one of the next generation of Tibetan leaders, a young woman named Kuzang Yuthok. Her grandfather had been the chief justice of Tibet and her father sometimes traveled with His Holiness the Dalai Lama as his interpreter. In 1959, she told me, her grandfather had fled Tibet with the Dalai Lama. That same year, Kuzang's mother, pregnant with Kuzang, was visiting India when the Chinese assault intensified; unable to return to Tibet, she gave birth to Kuzang in exile.

"I'm a true refugee kid," said Kuzang. Wearing a sweatshirt and her hair cut short, she looked like a young American. In a relaxed, West Coast way of speaking she said, "I was born in exile. I've never seen my country."

"Yet you're devoting your life to freeing Tibet?"

"Yes. Our people back in Tibet, they cannot speak for themselves. If they do, they will be imprisoned or killed. The rest of us out here are damned lucky. We're safe. We have enough to eat."

"And you are one of how many Tibetans in the United States?" I asked.

"Only five hundred so far. This year an-

During the summer months, these Tadjik people graze their goats and sheep on the high grasslands of China's western Himalayan plain. In fall, they pack all their belongings onto a single camel and descend to the relative warmth of the Taklomakan Desert.

other one thousand Tibetans will be allowed to settle in the United States. In America we're the minority of all minorities. But we do what we can for Tibet. We're preserving our culture here, teaching our children the language and all about our country, our history. Our culture lives with every one of us refugees, wherever we are."

One issue in particular troubled Kuzang as we spoke: Reports had come in that Tibetan women were being sterilized. Because the Red Cross, Amnesty International, and other human rights observers have been barred from Tibet, these reports have been difficult to document. However, Kuzang's aunt went into a clinic to have her child, and when she came out she was unable to conceive again. "It's hard to prove what happened," said Kuzang. "But we know there are mobile units that go from village to village, telling all the young Tibetan women to come out to be sterilized. Sometimes they give them a little bit of money to do it.

"The West has almost forgotten our story, but people are still dying in Tibet. They are being shot in the streets for demonstrating. They are being imprisoned for life just for unfolding a Tibetan flag."

"How long can your culture survive this way if the Chinese remain in control of Tibet?" I asked Kuzang.

"I have no idea. Hopefully, as long as there are Tibetans alive. But existing at what level? Culture is not just for individuals. It is for people, a community of people. . . ."

Kuzang paused for a moment, then continued more slowly. "We are not fighting to save Tibet only for Tibetans. Our Tibetan culture has much to offer the world. There are already many people in the West who are Tibetan Buddhists. Others find their own way to draw on our phi-

losophy, our way of life . . . our understanding of harmonious living. We can help others learn to value inner peace more than material wealth."

❖

Tibetans are but one of fifty-five minorities in today's China. Altogether, there are more than sixty-seven million indigenous people in China, about 7 percent of the overall population. They range from the Zhuang, who number ten million, to the Hezhe, of whom barely eight hundred exist. In the northern and western regions of Inner Mongolia, Xinjiang, and Tibet, the people breed animals and are nomadic pastoralists. In the southern regions, most of the indigenous peoples practice swidden cultivation, with a few still surviving by hunting and gathering.

Ironically, in the early 1900s China had a fairly enlightened policy for its indigenous peoples. After the founding of the Chinese Communist Party in 1922, native peoples were allowed a considerable degree of self-determination. However, in its prolonged struggle for power, the Chinese Communist Party began coveting the lands, rich with timber and minerals, of the indigenous peoples.

"As the Communists came closer to power, their attitudes towards the minorities were modified," writes Julian Burger, who coordinates the United Nations indigenous peoples program. "The principle of self-determination became subordinated to the overriding objective of building a socialist society throughout China."

Socialist reforms did raise the indigenous peoples' material standard of living, but during China's self-proclaimed "Great Leap Forward," from 1956 to 1958, the Communist Party began viewing indigenous customs as primitive obstacles to development and progress. In 1966, the Cultural Revolution mounted an intense assault on indigenous cultures, denying minority rights to self-determination, purging native leaders, and prohibiting the speaking, writing, and teaching of indigenous languages.

Today, the extreme persecution of indigenous peoples has given way to a more subdued policy of gradually assimilating the native peoples out of existence. But if they were to fade away, it would be the whole world's loss, not only China's. In the silenced voices of China's peoples lies a gentle wisdom that would help bring peace to the earth.

Young Wieger girls, Kashgar, China. The Wieger people live along the fabled Silk Road, which Mediterranean silk and spice traders used to travel over the Himalayas.

AINU

IN THE LAND OF HUMAN BEINGS

T hey are clothed in the bark of trees and the untanned skins of beasts," Isabela Bird wrote of the Ainu she saw on her 1878 trek to Nibutani, Japan. "They worship the bear, the sun, the moon, fire, water, and I know not what. . . . The obedience of their children is instantaneous. Gentle and peaceful as they are, they have a great admiration for fierceness and courage. . . . I hope I shall never forget the music of their low, sweet voices, the soft light of their mild brown eyes, and the wonderful sweetness of their smiles."

One hundred and fourteen years later, I was cruising along a well-paved road to Nibutani in a rented car. It was the first week of May, and there were patches of wild azaleas on the hillsides and, here and there, white flowers of the kobushi tree, said to foretell the next fall's harvest. The Saru River was running high with snow-melt waters from the mountains. The road crossed an expanse of once open mead-owland, which was now covered with ranches and estates of wealthy Japanese; their racehorses grazed in neatly fenced fields. I passed young Japanese couples on their way to a Cherry Blossom Festival and others playing golf on fairways flush with the first grass of spring.

Ainu in the Ainu language means "human being." This had been their land, Ainu-Moshir, the land of human beings. This northern island of Japan is now called Hokkaido, and as I could see from driving through the countryside, very little of it remains in the hands of the Ainu.

I arrived in Nibutani mid-morning and found my way along the shop-lined main street to a one-room log schoolhouse where Shiro Kayano directs an Ainu language program. His father, Shigeru Kayano, built this school as a place where Ainu children could learn about their culture. Today, there are about twenty-five thousand Ainu people, and perhaps three times more if one includes, as the Ainu do, everyone with a trace of Ainu blood. Fewer than a hundred still speak Ainu. At sixty-five, Shiro's father is one of the youngest.

Ainu children, Hokkaido, Japan.

"We started building this nursery school in 1980," Shiro said. "My father tried to teach Ainu to small children, but a government ministry opposed it and threatened to close the nursery school. So we've paid for things ourselves."

"Why doesn't the government help?" I asked.

"They must fear revival of the Ainu language, which they thought was dead," he said. "The Japanese would be very happy if our culture disappeared. So many things have already changed—our traditional dwellings, food, clothing. But if we speak our language, it survives, and the values of our culture will be preserved."

Like other early people of the North Pacific, the Ainu survived by hunting bear, deer, and wild birds; fishing for salmon and trout; and gathering greens and other edible plants. In place of a written language, they developed a rich oral tradition that reflects a close kinship with nature. "To the sea that nourishes us," goes an old Ainu salutation, "to the forest that protects us, we present our grateful thanks. You are two mothers that nourish the same child; do not be angry if we leave one to go to the other. The Ainu will always be the pride of the forest and of the sea."

In the valleys and mountains of Ainu-Moshir, the Ainu communicated with the *Kamui*, or spirits of all things. They looked upon the *Kamui* with great reverence and drew them into their lives in a worshipful way. When gathering plants in the mountains, they would pray to the spirit of the mountain. When cutting a tree, they would seek the understanding of the spirit of the woods. They particularly esteemed bears for their fierceness of spirit. When an Ainu caught a bear, it was occasion for celebration—people sang and danced, told stories, and gave prayers of thanks to send the bear's spirit back to the gods.

"We know that cultures perish. And once they disappear, there's no way to dig them up again," said Shiro. "I believe that cultures belong to the whole world. To keep our Ainu culture isn't just for us or the Japanese—it enriches the world. So to me the most important thing in life

is to protect our culture, until the day that many people appreciate it."

I asked him if the point was to regain Ainu land and other rights that the government denied.

"That's our hope. But first we must fight for recognition of our existence as a people. There are those among us who want the Japanese to pack up and leave Ainu-Moshir. But the majority of us simply want to be recognized as a separate people within the Japanese nation."

The Ainu have never been a nation in the modern sense. Historically, they were a fiercely independent tribal people who lived in small communities set about the land in a manner in balance with the woods and wild game. The first threat to their inherent sovereignty came in the sixteenth century, when clan lords moved in to monopolize the trade in salmon and furs. Soon, Japanese merchants were setting up trading posts and forcing the Ainu into a form of feudalistic slavery. Young men were made to labor without pay. Young Ainu girls were kept as maids and for the sexual gratification of their Japanese masters.

"Our people have been so deeply shamed," said Shiro, "that only a third of us live openly as Ainu. Another third of our people will acknowledge being Ainu only after much prodding. And the rest will never admit to being Ainu. The hardships my ancestors experienced are common to all Ainu. I'll tell you about my family."

At the time we talked, Shiro Kayano was thirty-four, a tall, sturdy man with a warm, engaging face. He had earned a university degree and held a professional job in a city, but he left and returned to Nibutani to help his people. "My children are Ainu," he said, "and they will grow up as Ainu. Seeing the Ainu way of life near at hand, it will be easier for them to have pride in being Ainu. In this sense they are lucky."

Shiro's father, Shigeru, was born at a time when the government made many Ainu fearful of speaking their own language. Nevertheless, he learned to speak Ainu from his grandmother. As a young man, he tried to fit into Japanese society,

In Nibutani, Japan, Shigeru Kayano, Ainu author and activist, stands next to a traditional Ainu dwelling he built as part of an indigenous peoples museum.

serving in the army before taking a job in forestry. Then, in his forties, he "woke up" to the fact that the Ainu culture was disappearing.

"My father saved all of our family's extra money to buy a tape recorder," said Shiro. "This was such an expensive thing for him to buy, I didn't understand then the importance of what he was doing. You see, with no written language, our people were superb storytellers. The stories contained all the wisdom of our people. My father has now recorded more than five hundred hours of Ainu stories that would have been lost."

Shigeru became a one-man task force for cultural survival. He wrote more than a dozen books about the Ainu people and used his modest savings to purchase old Ainu tools, crafts, clothing, and works of art so they wouldn't be lost to future generations. Eventually, he built a small museum and several old-style thatched houses. "Only now," said Shiro, "do I understand how devoted my father has been to preserving our culture."

A generation earlier, Shiro's grandfather had been arrested when he defied the Japanese ban prohibiting Ainu from catching salmon, a traditional staple in the Ainu diet. And a generation before that, in 1850, Shiro's great-grandfather, Tokkaram, had been one of those taken away by Samurai warriors—they had come to his

village and told the Ainus, under threat of death, to give over anyone who could work. From the one hundred and sixteen villagers, they had taken forty-three young men and women to work without pay in fishing camps and trading posts.

"My great-grandfather was only twelve years old when they led him off to work in a fish camp," said Shiro. "He longed for his family. Thinking he might be sent home if he were injured, he decided to cut off one of his fingers with a kitchen knife. He put his finger on the cutting board, but he couldn't bear to do it. The next day he went back to the cutting board, closed his eyes, and sliced off his left index finger. He screamed in pain. The Japanese foreman rushed in. But instead of letting him go home, the foreman said, 'Only a finger or two. It will heal easily if you put salt on it.'

"When Tokkaram's wound healed, he still wanted to go home so badly that he took the liver from a poisonous globe fish and smeared it over his body. His skin turned yellow. Thinking he was diseased, the foreman sent him home."

A Kayano family photograph shows an old man with the index finger missing on his left hand. "All the Ainu people have similar experiences in their families," said Shiro. "The Japanese government is responsible for letting these things happen, but it has never apologized. It hasn't even acknowledged that these things happened."

Shiro asserts that Japanese treatment of the Ainu people has been deliberately hidden from the mainstream of Japanese society and the rest of the world. The Ainu see 1699 as a turning point. Their strongest leader, Shakushain, tried to drive out the Japanese. When the decisive battle came, his men, armed only with bows and hunting weapons, held their own against the guns and Samurai of the Japanese. Shakushain was invited to peace negotiations, but at a dinner during the talks, he was assassinated. Ainu in outlying areas continued to live in relative freedom, but their leader's death effectively halted the development of an independent Ainu nation.

By the mid-eighteenth century, merchants

An early-twentieth-century Ainu couple. Only a few of the oldest women still have the traditional lip tattoos.

from the main island were tightening their grip on the Ainu. Their desire to increase profits led to a new level of cruelty and mistreatment—Ainu were beaten, robbed, and threatened with death if they refused to work. In 1789, a group of Ainu launched another unsuccessful revolt. After persuading them to surrender, the Japanese publicly beheaded thirty-seven Ainu men; their heads were pickled and packed off in barrels to go on display at a government outpost.

In 1868, the feudal trading empire gave way to the Meiji restoration. An imperial edict soon proclaimed that "the flourishing condition of Imperial Power is dependent upon the colonization and exploitation of Hokkaido." A newly formed Colonization Commission stepped up the immigration of Japanese to Ainu-Moshir. The remaining Ainu lands were confiscated and the Ainu people were stripped of their ethnic

identity. Forced to assume Japanese family names, they were classified as "former aborigines." They were forbidden to speak their native tongue or to hold traditional ceremonies. Deer and salmon became scarcer as wave after wave of Japanese settlers arrived. In 1873, 33 percent of the people on Ainu-Moshir were Ainu; just forty years later the Ainu would account for less than 1 percent of the population.

"The Ainu are an unenlightened people, backward, inferior, and doomed to disappear," proclaimed a Japanese official, reflecting the sentiment at the turn of the century. "Therefore we, the Japanese, full of chivalry, have to protect them by all means."

Protection came in the form of the Hokkaido Former Aborigine Protection Act of 1899, which, for all its altruistic claims, was an attempt to legislate the Ainu out of existence.

Rather than protecting their hunting and fishing rights, the Protection Act tried to turn the Ainu into farmers. Each Ainu household was granted about forty acres of land, but there was a catch: If they failed to cultivate their land, it would be confiscated. And the most productive lands had already gone to Japanese immigrants, leaving the Ainu the steeper slopes, marshes, floodplains, and other lands barely suitable for farming. One after another, Ainu families lost their lands to unscrupulous Japanese and drifted into the lowest economic strata. To survive after World War II, many had to leave Hokkaido for the casual labor markets of the big cities on the main island of Honshu.

"Why don't the Japanese people force the government to make amends for these past atrocities?" I asked Shiro. "Don't they know what happened?"

"Nobody knows, except for the few who make an effort to know," he said. "For the most part, the Japanese are blindfolded from the truth. If you go to Tokyo, you'll find that most people there know nothing at all about the Ainu."

❖

Prejudice against the Ainu pervaded Japanese society, and as Japanese immigrants poured into Hokkaido, it overwhelmed the Ainu. In the span of a hundred years, the Japanese population on the island rose from about twenty thousand to more than five million.

"We've been denied our dignity, starved spiritually, and left to grope about in Japanese society," said Chikap Mieko, a forty-four-year-old Ainu woman from Kushiro and living in Sapporo. She wore a dark-blue kimono she had embroidered with intricate Ainu designs, and her thick, dark hair floated down over her shoulders. "Our language is different," she said. "Our customs and habits are different, our way of looking at things is different, our values are different. Everything we have differs from the Japanese. And for being different, we're persecuted. Not only do they call us dirty and ugly, they make it almost

impossible for us to get good jobs. And many Japanese parents don't want an Ainu to marry into their families. The Japanese think we are subhuman. But we are human beings, like everyone else. I am an Ainu and am proud of it. But there are still a lot of us who want to hide who we are. Sometimes it feels very lonely to be Ainu."

Chikap explained that, along with her political battles for Ainu rights, the traditional *ikarakara* embroidery has become an expression of her Ainu identity. She first learned to embroider from her mother and later discovered that most of her people's *ikarakara* had been taken by "Ainu specialists" and put in museums. To develop her skills, Chikap had to visit museums to look at Ainu embroidery in glass showcases. She said that, "exhibited in this way, the Ainu culture seemed to be something long past. As a living Ainu, I felt my ancestry, my roots, were like a dream."

But from behind the glass, the old embroidery called to her: "You must make us into living *Kamui* again." Chikap explained that the embroidery she does comes from the time when Ainu daily life was inseparable from the *Kamui*, the spirits of the natural world. Doing the embroidery helps reestablish that relationship. Each stitch, loop, and knot breathes life into the threaded pattern, and eventually the intricate alchemy of her needlework turns the designs into living *Kamui*.

I asked Chikap if she thought that the Japanese and Ainu could learn to live together.

"I hope so," she said. "I hope we can. But it's going to be very difficult, because the government says there are no indigenous people in Japan. Our existence as Ainu, an indigenous people, is totally denied. But the reality is that we exist. We are the original people of this land. And we are not going to disappear."

"How could the government help you? What concrete changes would you like to see made?"

"The changes we need can't be realized in a few years. But starting the process of change is most important. The Japanese can start by being positive. Schools could invite older Ainu people into the classrooms to tell the story of our people, our culture, our customs, things like that, and to discuss human rights issues. But to begin this process of change, the government has to get rid of the 'Protection Act.' We need legislation that protects rather than strips away our human rights."

For more than two decades, the Ainu have tried to replace the Hokkaido Former Aborigine Protection Act with a law that recognizes their human rights. But this relic of nineteenth-century racism still forms the legal basis for Japanese relations with the Ainu and serves as a sort of psychological umbrella for a host of assimilationist attitudes and activities. This persistent and systematic attempt to assimilate the Ainu out of existence has set the Japanese on a collision course with the International Covenants on Human Rights. In 1979, the United Nations ratified these covenants, and the following year it called the Japanese government to task. The government tried to finesse its way around the violation of Ainu rights by attempting to deny their existence as indigenous people. Said one Japanese official to the U.N., "Ethnic minorities, as defined in this covenant, do not exist in Japan."

In 1986, Japanese Prime Minister Nakasone reaffirmed this policy: "Japan is a nation of homogeneous people." Then, in December 1991, the Japanese government finally admitted that the Ainu existed as an ethnic minority. But it still refused to acknowledge the fact that they are indigenous—a fact that would force the recognition of Ainu rights. And the most important right to most, if not all, indigenous people is their right to the land on which they have lived and evolved as a people.

Many Ainu have felt either too vulnerable to the government or too unsure of themselves to press their land claims aggressively. But Chikap Mieko, who seems to have been born an activist, is demanding that the so-called northern territories of Japan be returned to the Ainu, who his-

Chikap Mieko. "The government says there are no indigenous people in Japan. But the Ainu are still here. We exist. And we are not disappearing."

torically lived on the Kuril island chain. After World War II, Japan lost the Kurils to the Soviet Union. Japan is now trying to get them back, but the Russians are resisting. Ironically, the Japanese, who stole the Kurils from the Ainu, are now claiming with great indignation that Russia stole the Kurils from Japan. The Ainu are caught in the tug-of-war.

"The Russians have more understanding of our cause," said Chikap. "I think it's because they are multicultural. They not only recognize the Ainu as a distinct people, but realize that we have valid, historic rights to these northern territories. The Japanese government is refusing to involve Ainu people in the negotiations. But we must be involved. Our people used to live in the northern territories. They were our land. We need that land today. Because without land we can't recuperate, we can't rescue our culture and survive the next century. I want to help create a village on our land where young Ainu people can learn their traditional culture and lifestyle. We need our own land again, a place where we can be ourselves. This is my dream."

❖

Since returning to my home in Alaska, I have found myself wondering why the Japanese government doesn't simply say, "We made some mistakes with the Ainu. Now we'll make amends." Of course, governments rarely acknowledge their own errors.

As improbable as it may seem, I think the Japanese are afraid of the Ainu. It is not an armed uprising that they fear. Nor is it the cost of a land claims settlement. After all, in the war with Iraq they came up with $3 billion to help hand Kuwait back to the ruling sheiks. And I doubt if they are afraid that the Ainu language will replace Japanese.

The Japanese fear of the Ainu operates at deeper and murkier levels. Recognizing the Ainu as indigenous people would damage the Japanese myth of "sameness." And listening, really listening, to the pleas of the Ainu would mean admitting to their systematic attempts to eliminate them over more than three hundred years. The walls of denial are never easy to tear down, and doing so might be particularly difficult for the Japanese, given their preoccupation with honor and saving face.

But I suspect that, on an even deeper level, many Japanese are somewhat fearful of the wilder, nature-connected spirit of the Ainu because they are uncomfortable with this part of themselves.

"Connection with nature runs much deeper in Ainu culture than it does in that of the Japanese," Shiro Kayano told me in Nibutani. "We've seen the Japanese take as much as they can. What happens later, they don't care. They care only about how much money they make.

"But there are things more important than making money—generosity, kindly feelings toward the weak, broad-mindedness, caring for the earth. We have much to offer the Japanese."

"I wonder how many people appreciate that point?" I mused.

"Hardly any. Still, this is very important. In modern Japanese society, people want to have so many things, so many luxuries. This is the Japanese reality: not caring about the destruction of the environment of Japan or other countries. In our Ainu way of thinking, we take and use the minimum amount for necessities. The Ainu think that it's nature that conserves human beings, not the other way around. If we recognize the limits of nature and live within them, then nature will renew itself."

This is more than a domestic issue. In December 1992, Giichi Nomura, president of the Ainu Association, told the U.N. General Assembly that "the overseas activities of Japanese corporations and the foreign aid efforts of the Japanese government are having serious effects on the livelihood of indigenous peoples all over the world. This situation is linked to the indifference shown toward indigenous people within Japan.

"Through a new partnership," Nomura concluded hopefully, "we believe the government of Japan will come to realize its responsibilities, not just toward the Ainu, but toward all indigenous peoples."

SARAWAK

IN THE OLDEST FOREST

W hy me?" asked Mutang Urud as we walked along the waterfront in
Rio de Janeiro. He seemed to be asking himself as well as me. "Why
have I been thrust into the middle of all this? Why me?"

Virtually overnight, Mutang had gone from being a landscaper who loved
the simple pleasures of planting trees and shrubs to being an exiled leader of the
Kelabit Penan and twenty-three other indigenous peoples of Sarawak on the island
of Borneo in the country of Malaysia. During the Earth Summit in Rio de Janeiro
in the summer of 1992, Mutang and I passed many evenings sharing meals, taking
walks, and just staying up late and talking.

Mutang, who was a Kelabit tribesman, had just spent a month imprisoned
in solitary confinement for organizing resistance to the logging of his people's forest
lands. The rate of deforestation in Malaysia is the highest in the world. Existing
contracts call for the cutting of 73 percent of the remaining forest. The Malaysian
government maintains that its logging practices are "sustainable," but disinterested
forest managers fear that even if Sarawak's pace of logging is cut in half in 1993,
Sarawak's rain forest will still disappear by the end of the century.

When Mutang was first arrested, the government didn't give a reason, but
the people knew it was because he was seen as a leader of the Sarawak Indigenous
People's Alliance and supported the human barricades to block the logging trucks.

"Now I'm a wanted man in my own country," said Mutang. "There's a warrant out for my arrest. If I go back, I will be put in jail. When I was in detention, the
police told me, 'You must never do this again. We know all about you. You cannot
hide from us. We won't give you a second chance.'"

Mutang's predicament was at once simple and complex, both very personal
and inextricably linked to the fate of the native people of Sarawak. If he returned to
Sarawak, his lawyer said, he could expect to be in prison for nine years. Given the
unsanitary conditions and prospect of torture, he might never come out. Still, he
yearned to return to his homeland. Then again, it was possible that he would be far
more useful to his people if he stayed out of prison.

*One of several
hundred Penan
still living in the
rain forest of
Sarawak.*

Mutang Urud. "I was arrested for objecting to the logging that has already made thousands of us homeless and polluted 70 percent of Sarawak's rivers. How will our children and grandchildren survive?"

"I'm willing to go to prison if it encourages our people to rise up against the logging," he told me. "But will my being jailed stir them into action? Our people are naturally reserved, and now they are terrified of the soldiers and police. If I'm locked away, they might become even more discouraged. In exile, I could get information back to them and tell the world about our problems. But then again, maybe it would reinforce my people's courage if I sacrificed my freedom. It's very hard to know what to do."

"In Sarawak, you'll either be in jail or in hiding," I said, beginning to feel protective of Mutang's safety. "Either way could be dangerous."

"And the thing is," he answered, "I could avoid all these problems and have a very comfortable life back home—if I went along with the government's destruction of the forest. Timber companies have offered me lots of money to stop my organizing work. And the authorities have said to me, 'Join us. You'll have a good life, everything you want. Help us develop the country and pull these people out of the Stone Age. Why make

things difficult for yourself?'"

When Mutang refused to be bought off, the Malaysian government began following his every move. Before leaving Sarawak, he had to live undercover for two weeks, moving from house to house. To get through customs to go to Rio, he used a disguise. And before Mutang spoke at the Earth Summit, Malaysian authorities asked to meet with him. Instead of offering to drop the charges or change their policies, they warned him not to speak against the government.

Mutang didn't waver. He spoke out. But in a similar situation, many of Sarawak's indigenous peoples might have backed down; their cultures are by nature nonconfrontational and many native individuals consider the government's machinery too powerful to resist. Ironically, some of these cultures' most beautiful traits have contributed to their undoing. The Dyaks' tradition of welcoming visitors into their communities, for example, has helped expose them to those who came to exploit them. And their great reverence for elders has sometimes led them to respect government officials who don't have their interests at heart.

"Sometimes we are too trusting of the modern world," said Mutang. "We believe other people are as sincere as we are. We are learning the hard way that there are people who want to exploit us. The politicians are making use of our good will to convince some of our people to take jobs cutting trees so they can build good houses. But if the forest is logged, what will be left for my children and my grandchildren?

"In our race to modernize, our leaders must not blindly follow the path of Western economic development," cautioned Mutang. "Many people in the West have been uprooted from their traditions, their cultural roots. And this is my fear for my people. If we are pulled up from our roots, what happens? If you uproot a tree or a flower, it will die. I think a lot of people in the West have been uprooted and have become spiritual drifters. And I've seen spiritual drifters among indigenous peoples in Australia, Brazil, and North America. I see this trend among my people. And this makes me very sad."

To our Western eyes, Mutang is something of a paradox, combining traits we are not used to seeing together. He is one of the warmest and gentlest men I have ever met—thoughtful, respectful, even tender in his relations with others. But he also draws from a very deep well of courage. The turning point in his life came in 1984, when a large timber contractor began cutting on the traditional lands of the Penan and Dyak peoples. "Since then," he says, "life has never been the same for any of us."

With the pressure of logging and government threats mounting, Mutang felt the need to withdraw for a while to reflect on the crisis and the role he could play. He walked alone through the jungle for two days, climbing steep cliffs and crossing crocodile-infested rivers to reach a remote beach. There, at the edge of the forest, he used branches and vines to build a small hut. It was the monsoon season, and gale-force winds often blew apart his makeshift shelter.

"During the nights, the waves hit the cliffs and rocks so hard that they frightened me," said Mutang. "It was raining hard. There was thunder. Lightning threw eerie silhouettes onto the forest canopy. I was at the crossroads of my life. I'd wake early in the morning and lie there thinking about how there are things more important than earning money and being comfortable. I prayed for guidance. I wanted to grapple with the fear within myself—a fear of darkness and the unknown, fear of the government and the loggers, fear of the future and all the uncertainties of life."

When Mutang returned from his time alone, he firmly resolved to commit his life to saving his people's homeland, which is in the heart of what many scientists consider the earth's most ancient forest. This extraordinary web of trees, vines, shrubs, and flowers represents the ebb and flow of some one hundred sixty million years of evolution. In terms of trees alone, Sarawak has the richest forest in the world. In an area slightly smaller than New York State, several

thousand species of trees live along with twenty thousand kinds of flowering plants, several hundred varieties of butterflies, and nearly two hundred species of mammals. To enter this forest realm is like walking back into the dawn of time, for sequestered here in the soft light beneath the trees are people who still live with an intimate connection to the subtle stirrings of the forest.

"Down there in our longhouses in the trees my people live in the most wonderful homeland anyone could have," Mutang told me. "The forest provides shelter, food, and medicine and holds the history of our people—our myths, our legends, and stories. If we walked the forest trails together, I would be able to show you at every turn what had happened here, who had been hunting over there, everything. That grove of trees might be where I was almost bitten by a wild pig. I could take you to a tree marked by my uncle, who is now dead. The lives of our people are written in the landscape. And we know every tree and turn of the creeks. In cities I get lost easily, but out there in the forest I always know where I am. We have names for thousands of streams and creeks, even the smallest trickles."

However, when the Malaysian authorities look at the forests of Sarawak, they see not a diversity of species and the pathways of a people, but an enormous storehouse of wealth. This perspective is hardly surprising, for the forest has never been their home. And historically Sarawak is not their country but a territory that fell into their laps with the collapse of colonialism. When Malaysia claimed Sarawak, it took possession of the earth's last substantial stands of the magnificent *dipterocarp* hardwood trees that grow to a hundred and fifty feet in height and many yards in circumference. By the mid 1980s, this region, which is less than one-tenth the size of the Amazonian rain forest, was exporting more than half of all the whole-log tropical timber in the world.

"Logging has been my bread and butter since I was a pioneer in the industry in 1949," says Sarawak's Minister of Environment and Tourism, Datuk Amar James Wong. "I can be held responsible for damage caused by logging but my conscience is clear." The apparent paradox in Wong's untroubled conscience may reflect his desire for progress, development, and modernity. "If every longhouse wants a communal forest," he notes, "we might as well stop logging. They [the Penan] should give way to the needs of the country."

But to Sarawak's indigenous peoples, the logging is a systematic destruction of their country. First the forest is cut, then plantations are developed that prevent the native people from pursuing their traditional hunting and gathering. To complete the undercutting of the local communities, nearly all the logging profits are siphoned off and invested in the United States and Europe. Sarawak's Chief Minister, Taib Mahmud, has given many of the lucrative logging contracts to his political allies and family members. Mahmud's personal wealth is estimated at $4 billion U.S., and stands in stark contrast to the native villages, which lack basic sanitation services, adequate food and medical care, and clean water supplies.

One of the most tragic human as well as environmental consequences of the logging has been the contamination of 70 percent of Sarawak's rivers and streams. Not only have trucks and bulldozers muddied the waters with sediment, but poisons in the bark of fallen trees have found their way into the waterways and killed the fish. As fish, birds, and small mammals disappear from logged areas, the Penan and other Dyak people lose their traditional sources of food and can no longer live by roving through the forest. Many of them are now crowded into squalid camps, where they are succumbing to parasitic infections, dysentery, tuberculosis, and rheumatic fever. In many settlements, virtually every child has been afflicted with impetigo, scabies, and other skin diseases. Up to 50 percent of the children suffer some degree of malnutrition.

"It is not true that we don't want progress," says a Penan woman. "We want schools and clinics. But give us our customary rights to the land first. Stop logging, and then we can decide on development at our own pace."

"This house the government gave us is good," says a relocated Penan, "but it is useless if we have no food. We want to fish and hunt. Tourists see the new house and think we are happy. We are not. First we want our forest. We want to be Penan."

Malaysian officials contend that there are only a few hundred nomadic Penan left in the forest, too few, they say, to warrant special attention. But in addition to the Penan, there are hundreds of thousands of other indigenous people who still depend upon the forest. The government believes that these people should be joining the modern world. "We'd like to take them out of the jungle. Give them a decent modern living," said Mrs. Rafidah Aziz, Malaysia's Minister of International Trade and Industry in May 1992. When queried about opposition to logging in Sarawak, she said, "It has nothing to do with logging, actually. It's got to do with the existence of what was originally six thousand members of the Penan tribe who were for a long time living in the tropical forests of Sarawak. . . . Now at this point there are about three hundred odd of these Penan still resisting to come out of the jungle. . . . I mean we're talking about 1992. We're talking about the twenty-first century. We cannot afford to have some of our population still hunting monkeys."

Mrs. Aziz responded strongly to a British television program that showed a Penan woman reacting with alarm to the disappearance of wildlife in the forest. It was getting harder and harder, said the woman, for her children to find monkeys or other meat. "Big deal!" said Mrs. Aziz. "The Europeans in England are saying that this woman is being deprived of a decent livelihood. I mean, she talks about children going to shoot monkeys. *We're* talking about children using computers. . . . People still shooting monkeys. Big deal! Some people actually believe this is the way these people should live. No schools. No nothing. Let them go walking around in a loin cloth. . . . We have this [fascination for] exotic tribal life. Therefore don't

Penan tribesmen. "The forest is our home and friend for thousands of years, but now they are destroying it without heart and feelings for our lives. What we want is our survival, a place to continue our culture and traditions, and to see that our grandchildren have a future."

touch this and don't touch their cultural heritage, their burial grounds, and so on. And therefore stop logging. That is *sick*."

In March 1992, a handwritten note smuggled out from the Penan deep in the Sarawak forest told a different story. "We would like to send messages to all the world who are in support of our struggle to halt the logging," wrote Penan leaders, who for ten months had been with Mutang on the logging road blockade. "The Malaysian authorities say that foreigners have no rights to protect our forests. But we believe in you and hope you will help us."

The Penan message to the world went on to say that when the riot police came with helmets, weapons, and tear gas to break up the blockade, "there were only a few of us at the blockade. If we continued to stay we would be killed. . . . The Malaysian authorities say that we have no rights to these lands. But our people have always been living in Sarawak. We have rights. We look to you in the outside world to assist us in our struggle. If you do not assist us, soon we will die in the hands of the Malaysian authorities."

❖

After the Earth Summit in Brazil, Mutang Urud resolved his agonizing decision by choosing to live in exile in Canada. When I called to talk with him, he said, "I realized that I could help my people more from out here. I can get them the most current information and put them in touch with others who want to help. This will make them aware and strengthen their resolve. And I can also prepare myself for the day when I finally return home to my country."

In exile, Mutang was separated from his family and could not join his people in blockading the logging roads. But he could try to reason with other countries that are extinguishing his people by buying so much timber from Sarawak. Japan is the worst offender. With about 2 percent of the world's population, it has become the world's leading importer of tropical hardwoods. More than 90 percent of Japan's hardwood log

imports come from the Malaysian states of Sarawak and Sabah. Most of these logs are pressed into plywood, used once or twice for concrete forms, and then discarded.

Mutang traveled to Japan to appeal to Prime Minister Miyazawa and other chief ministers. He explained how in areas that are logged, the fish, wild animals, birds, sago palms, and medicinal plants disappear. He described how hundreds of his people's graveyards have been bulldozed away. He said, "We have done everything in our power to bring these issues to the attention of our government and the logging companies, but these appeals have fallen on deaf ears. That is why I have been forced to come to Japan, which is the number one importer of timber from Sarawak. As long as you continue to buy timber from our lands, you are directly involving yourselves in the destruction of our livelihood, tradition, and culture."

When Mutang makes such public statements, Malaysian officials usually go to great lengths to try to discredit him. Ironically, he could be their greatest ally. If people like Sarawak's Chief Minister Taib Mahmud maintain their present policies, history will judge them harshly. What others have tried to do with guns and gas chambers, these policy makers are inadvertently doing with chain saws and bulldozers. The extermination of a people is extermination, no matter how it is done. Rather than plunging ahead with logging practices that are extinguishing the Penan and other indigenous peoples, the Malaysian officials could take the lead in finding ways to balance resource development with the preservation of native lifestyles.

❖

The next time I saw Mutang he was at the global meeting that inaugurated 1993 as the Year of the Indigenous People at the United Nations in New York. When his moment came, Mutang rose, walked to the podium of the General Assembly, looked out over the great ampitheater of nations, and said, "The Malaysian government says that it is bringing us progress and development. But all we see are dusty logging roads and relocation camps. For us, their so-called progress means only starvation, dependence and helplessness, the destruction of our culture, and the demoralization of our people. The government says it is creating jobs for our people. But these jobs will disappear along with the forest.

"A high government official once told me that in order to have development, someone must make a sacrifice. Why should it be us who must make this sacrifice? We have already given so much. We have already become poor and marginalized. Now there is nothing left for us to sacrifice except our lives.

"For defending our way of life, we have been called greenies, traitors, and terrorists. Our lives are threatened by company goons. Our women are raped by loggers who invade our villages. While the companies get rich from our forests, we are condemned to live in poverty."

Mutang paused for a moment. His voice cracked with emotion. "Must people die before you respond? Must there be war and blood running in the streets before the United Nations will come to a people's assistance? Even though we are desperate, our people have avoided violence. We have used only peaceful methods of protest. Why does this organization, which is dedicated to peace, not listen to the pleas of a peaceful people?"

Two Penan men pause to roast a fish.

SOUTHEAST ASIA

THE TEARS OF OUR PEOPLE

A Toda woman of the Nilgiri Hills in southern India.

*T*here is no point in trying to make them a second-rate copy of ourselves," India's Prime Minister Jawaharlal Nehru once said of his country's indigenous peoples. "They are people who sing and dance and try to enjoy life, not people who sit in stock exchanges, shout at each other, and think themselves civilized. . . . We do not mean to interfere with their way of life, but want to help them live it . . . according to their own genius and tradition."

In 1950, under Nehru's guidance, India adopted a policy of protection for its tribal peoples. But in the push to modernize India, this vision of a multicultural society has been difficult to achieve. Some tribes, although quite small, have been subjected to various measures of population control. And when there is a dam to be built, a forest developed, or a park established, tribal peoples have often been forced from their homes and relocated.

"When we lived in the hills, we had everything we needed," said Goga Gaita, an elder of the Bartars, after the government had moved his people. "Our forefathers lived in the hills. They had their gods, their prayers, and their land. We had a happy life there. We had enough to eat. And nobody bothered us. But the new land we came to twenty years ago doesn't bring us luck or enough to eat. Three years ago, government people came and sterilized all our married men. Since then we are getting fewer and fewer. Our gods have left us and the land doesn't want us either."

In northern India, the last villages of Banjara people are being crowded out of existence. Centuries ago, some of the Banjara began migrating westward across and then out of India, through the Middle East to Europe, and eventually to the United States. Although they did physical labor when they had to, they preferred to survive as performers and fortune tellers. In time, they became known as gypsies.

In the Nilgiri Hills of southern India lived four groups of tribal people whose isolation, until recently, afforded them some protection. The Toda, Kota, Badagas, and Kurumba people long lived in peace on a temperate plateau six thousand feet above the muggy lowlands, trading and bartering with each other. But when the British built a road to their region, alien values and customs upset the age-old balance. The Badagas, who were farmers, began merging with the mainstream culture of southern India. But the Kota, who were musicians and artists, and the reclusive Kurumba, known as woodsmen and sorcerers, could not adapt, and today these groups have all but disappeared. The Toda, whose lives revolve around their buffalo, are down to about three hundred families. Desperately, this remnant is trying to hold onto its customs and spiritual beliefs.

"Ours is a sad story," Evam Pilgain told photographer John Isaac and me. "Many outsiders are moving to Todaland and we may lose our rights."

Now in her sixties, Evam is a remarkable woman who had to overcome illiteracy, custom, and the traditional caste and gender bias of India to become a highly revered leader of the Toda

A Toda mother and child. Among the Toda, women are allowed more than one "husband."

people. As a child, she told me, she played the role of Florence Nightingale in a school play; in a flash of self-discovery, she knew she was meant to become a nurse. She studied hard and in time managed to finish her training in London, where she enjoyed her new life. She might well have remained there had not an alarming report on the decline of the Toda people come to her. For several days, she could neither eat nor sleep, and within two weeks she was on her way back to India.

But there were no jobs for a nurse in the Nilgiri Hills. So for more than a year, Evam lived off her savings and volunteered her services. Then, at a meeting in Madras, she met Prime Minister Nehru. She told him that she had returned to help her people—just as he had encouraged young educated people to do—but could find no employment. She soon received an appointment as the region's head nurse.

A few years later, Nehru came to the Nilgiris on vacation and visited Evam. He asked her about the Toda's marriage practices, a matter, he told Evam, that troubled him deeply. Then, as now, when a Toda girl was born, her parents arranged for her betrothal. At about fifteen, she moved to the chosen boy's home and married not only him but his younger brothers as well. Two months before her first child was born, one of her husbands, usually the eldest brother, would present her with a symbolic bow and arrow and proclaim himself the child's official father. The identity of the child's biological father remained unimportant. Later, with the consent of her husbands, she could take another Toda man to be her lover.

"This freedom, this having more than one man, troubles me," Nehru admitted to Evam. "What are you going to do about these marriage customs in this modern age?"

"Nothing, sir," Evam replied.

"Why not?" countered the Prime Minister.

"Because we are only doing openly what many so-called civilized people do in secret. We

An indigenous woman in India, which has fifty-one million indigenous people belonging to more than two hundred tribal groups.

are more honest. Why should I try to make our people dishonest?"

As Evam recalls, Nehru thought for a moment, and then, without another word, broke into a wide grin and thrust his hand forward.

When John Isaac and I spoke with Evam in the spring of 1993, Nehru had, of course, long since passed away, and the encroachment of civilization was presenting the Toda with new difficulties. A film company that had moved to the region was dumping chemical wastes on Toda lands. Following the example of Mahatma Gandhi, Evam told us, she went to the site and performed *satyagraha*, fasting and praying, trying to persuade the company, by appealing to its conscience, to clean up after itself. She succeeded.

Evam was well aware that her people were few and their problems many, but she was quick to reject any suggestion that her people were vanishing. "Only last year," she said, "a scholar from the United States came to study us, and before leaving he said that the Toda people were going to gradually vanish. I opposed him. I asked, 'What makes a person a Toda or any other tribe? Not the dress. Not the jewelry. For us it is the sacred buffalo. The Toda are a Buffalo people.'"

Every stage of Toda life—from birth through childhood and adulthood and on to the afterlife—is marked by a rite of passage involving the sacred buffalo. When a child is conceived, buffalo milk is used in a ceremony to legitimize it. The first public showing of an infant's face occurs near the temple, which is illuminated with lamps burning *ghee*, a form of buffalo butter. And when a Toda dies, a buffalo is sacrificed.

"Perhaps there are now living only three hundred Toda families. We still all know each buffalo's name and can trace the genealogy of our herds for ten generations. Our main temple has not been closed for thousands of years, and the lamps that burn buffalo *ghee* there are always lit. When the temple is closed and all our ceremonies stop, *then* I will say the Toda have vanished. Only then."

❖

The Toda are bound to face new challenges, but ironically they are among the most secure of Southeast Asia's one hundred and fifty million indigenous people. In Vietnam, the survival of the tribal people is challenged not only

A Banjara woman of Hyderabad, India. Gypsy people throughout the world can trace their lineage back to Banjara tribespeople of India, who are now losing what remains of their homeland.

by modernity but by the lingering effects of the war, napalm bombing, and chemical defoliation of their land. In Cambodia, tribal people have borne the excesses of the Khmer Rouge in an area that has come to be known as "the killing fields." And in Afghanistan, the Soviet occupation displaced most of the country's indigenous people. According to the United Nations, six million Afghanis became refugees—a third of the nation's people and nearly half the world's estimated refugee population.

Elsewhere, many of Asia's indigenous people have been engulfed by the exploding populations of more dominant cultures. Taiwan, for example, was once inhabited only by indigenous people. Even today, eleven distinct tribes—more than three hundred and thirty thousand people—can be found on the island, but they account for only 1.7 percent of the total population.

In contrast, the people of the tiny Andaman Islands in the Bay of Bengal, midway between India and Burma, have suffered in isolation. The largest tribe, the Great Andamanese, numbered about four thousand in 1858, when the British established a penal colony on their island. Today, disease and ill-fated battles with the English have reduced the native population to fewer than thirty individuals of mixed ancestry. On the most isolated Andaman island, about a hundred and fifty Negrito people, none of them more than five feet tall, have pretty much held their own against the twentieth century. They are known to shoot arrows at intruders when they arrive and have been seen dancing when they leave.

In Bangladesh and Myanmar (Burma), the indigenous peoples have managed to retain no such strongholds. All of them have become pawns in the brutal struggles of their regions' ethnic and religious zealots. Of all the world's people, the Chakma, Tripura, Karen, Mon, and a number of smaller tribal groups in this region face the most blatant forms of genocide.

❖

"Suddenly we were standing in water, then trying to swim in the flood," said a man from the Chittagong Hills of Bangladesh. To disguise his identity he wore dark glasses. He sat cross-legged on the ground next to me and explained how the Kaptai Dam had uprooted a hundred thousand of his people.

"We had no warning. One day they closed the gates of the dam and the water started rising. There were children and women who couldn't swim. Many of them drowned. My entire family was uprooted. We think of the water in the lake as the tears of our people."

"Did anyone in your family die?"

"No, my brother, my sister, and my mother fled to India and are now living in a refugee camp. I lost everything. I no longer have any land or a home. I'm like a floating man. And my people have become voiceless. We cannot speak out. We have lost everything. We are even losing our courage."

He spoke in quick bursts, as if we might be interrupted at any moment. He was a leader of the Chakma, Marma, Tripura, and ten other tribal peoples who are indigenous to the Chittagong Hill Tracts in Bangladesh. We met in a secure location, and I agreed not to identify him. Were officials in his country to learn of our conversation, he could have been assassinated.

For a while he talked about his love of the simple, unassuming life his people used to enjoy in the Chittagong Hills, which are still home to six hundred thousand tribal people. Long ago, they learned how to scratch out a meager but sustainable living by farming the hills of their homeland. But in 1963, the Kaptai Dam not only uprooted many of their people, it flooded 40 percent of their farmable land. This proved

Indigenous musicians of Navikotava, India.

An adivasis, or tribesman, of India, with his grandson. Fewer than 15 percent of India's tribal people have access to schools and health care.

to be just one in a series of tragedies that has marked the twentieth century for the Chittagong Hill people.

During Britian's colonial rule of India, the Chittagong people were relatively undisturbed. In 1900, the British even assured them that outsiders would not be allowed to settle in their region. But when India won its independence from Britian in 1947, their troubles began. As the British empire splintered apart, the Chittagong region became a bargaining chip. Since the Chittagong people were predominantly Christian and Buddhist, it would have been logical for their territory to have remained a part of India. But Calcutta, with its sizable Muslim population, went to India; so as a trade-off, the Chittagong Hill people were spun

off to Pakistan, with whose Muslim Bengali people they had no cultural or religious ties.

Pakistan was soon engaged in a bloody civil war. Muslims from neighboring districts started moving into the Hill Tracts, and the Pakistan Army helped them take lands from the tribal people. When the war ended, a new country had been established—Bangladesh. The Hill people asked this new government to return the lands taken by Pakistan. In response, Bangladesh unleashed its military to confiscate even more tribal lands.

In a typical attack in the spring of 1977, Bangladesh soldiers plundered four villages, marched fifty-four men into a pit and shot them, and raped and tortured to death twenty-three women. Three days before Christmas in 1978, soldiers burned twenty-two villages to the ground. They then arrested all the males ages fifteen to seventeen in the village of Gargajyachar and cut them to pieces with their own broad knives. By the end of 1978, the government of Bangladesh had maimed or killed thirty thousand tribal people.

Despite these attacks, the tribal people still made up 90 percent of the region's population. But in 1979, the military assault was coupled with a transmigration program. In the span of only five years, Bangladesh sent four hundred thousand Muslim settlers into the Hill Tracts. Overnight, the tribal people became a minority, and many of the newly arrived settlers started looting their villages.

"A reign of terror is prevailing in the entire area," reported Uprendra Lal Chakma, a leader of the Hill people. "The evicted tribal people do not dare come back to their destroyed and demolished villages. Harassment, manslaughtering, arson, looting, and threats from the settlers continue."

The effects of the military-backed transmigration remained all but hidden from the outside world. While Bangladesh encouraged

Muslim settlers with land grants, cash, and rations, it repeatedly assured the United Nations that it had no program of sponsored migration. This conspiracy to extinguish the tribal cultures continued through the 1980s.

"On May 1, 1986, settlers came and captured my land," recounts a Chakma refugee. "Soldiers helped them burn our houses. The whole village of sixty houses was burnt. After seeing this, we ran through the jungle and eventually reached India."

"About fifty army personnel rounded up the whole village," recalls a thirty-year-old woman refugee. "All our men were arrested. They stripped me naked and tied up my hands and legs. Then they raped me in front of my father-in-law. Three other girls were raped in front of me."

For more than twenty years, the world learned of such events only from those who had already fled the country. In the spring of 1991, the Chittagong Hill Tracts Commission dispatched the first independent fact-finding mission to the region. It reported that "Hill people are being killed, tortured, raped, injured, and arrested. . . . The army is enforcing a system of Bengali culture and administration onto the Hill people. It has become extremely difficult for the Hill people to retain their own specific identities and has even made the possibility of physical survival perilous. . . . A genocidal process still threatens the Hill people."

A year after the commission's report was released, I met with the Chakma leader. His people had just been hit by the biggest massacre in eighteen years.

"We learned about it on April 11, when we gathered to celebrate our culture. We had invited nonindigenous people—lawyers, judges, journalists, political leaders, anybody interested— to join our cultural event. We wanted to show them how we lived. But when we heard what had happened the day before, we could not celebrate.

A survivor told me that Bengali settlers and soldiers had killed more than twelve hundred people. They locked them inside their own homes and set fire to their houses. Just burned them up.

"But we are unable to express our outrage. We don't dare. Just for organizing peaceful activities, many of our leaders have been shot or are under arrest. Some of our people went underground and have been fighting for as long as eighteen years. They don't have any choice. They had to take up arms to protect their families."

"And you?" I asked him.

"I am a democratic activist, but with the military controlling our lives, how can we practice democracy? We are living in a police state, a war zone. Our whole area is under military occupation. They have one soldier for every seven of our people. If I were living in my home area, I wouldn't last long. But I often go to my area to see my people. I go in different disguises."

Since 1971, more than fifty thousand Hill people have fled to India. Those who stayed were uprooted from their ancestral land and forced to live in "cluster villages," patrolled and controlled by the military. Meanwhile, the Bangladesh government remains dependent on foreign aid from the United States, Japan, and other developed countries, and from agencies such as the World Bank and the Asian Development Bank.

"What is this aid used for?" asked the Chakma leader, shaking his head. "We are not bloody fools. The foreign aid supports the government's policy of exterminating our people. The foreign aid supports the raping of our wives and daughters, the killings, burning of houses, destroying of villages, occupation of our lands, transmigration, everything . . ." He paused a moment. Then: "I lost my house. It was destroyed by the military."

"And your family? Are your wife and girls safe?"

"My wife, my little girls . . ." He searched for words and then began crying uncontrollably, sobbing, his broad shoulders shaking. "I don't know. I don't know. I have to believe they are still alive."

After a moment he composed himself.

"I don't understand the Bangladesh government," he said with dignity. "We are not terrorists. We are fighting for our existence. Why are they driving us to extinction?"

❖

East of Bangladesh lies Burma, a country about the size of Texas. Its forty-two million people speak more than a hundred languages. With its rich soils, hardwood forests, oil, jade, rubies, and sapphires, Burma was once the wealthiest country in Southeast Asia. But now it is one of the poorest, its prosperity drained by a prolonged civil war that has driven millions of Karen, Mon, and other tribal people into poverty and exile.

Once a British colony, Burma won its independence in 1948 with the help of Aung San, a brilliant and charismatic young man who united in the struggle for democracy most of his country's more than one hundred and thirty ethnic groups. Aung San envisioned a Burma in which the indigenous minorities would be full partners. But while writing a constitution for the newly independent nation, Aung San was assassinated. Having lost the one man who could unify the disparate cultural factions, Burma fell into an abyss of repression and armed revolution from which it has yet to emerge.

The military and secret police became a privileged class, while indigenous leaders organized their resistance forces in the highlands and ran their governments in exile. On August 8, 1988, tens of thousands of people marched in the streets of Burma's capital, Rangoon, to plead peacefully for a democratic government. The military opened fire on the demonstrators. Hundreds died. Protests spread throughout the countryside. The military struck back in the guise of the State Law and Order Restoration Council,

known as SLORC. In the following weeks, more than five thousand children, students, workers, housewives, and monks were shot.

During that pivotal summer of 1988, a remarkable woman returned to her Burma homeland, inspiring a sense of hope in a country that had plunged into chaos. She was Aung San Suu Kyi, daughter of Burma's beloved Aung San, who had won freedom for Burma forty years before. Suu Kyi had been two years old when her father was killed. Although she had gone on to study, marry, and raise two children in England, she remained close to her people. "She constantly reminded me that one day she would have to return to Burma," writes her husband, Michael Aris, in the introduction to her book *Freedom from Fear*. "From her earliest childhood, Suu has been deeply preoccupied with the question of what she might do to help her people."

Her opportunity came unexpectedly in the summer of 1988. When her mother suffered a stroke, Suu Kyi rushed back to Rangoon. While caring for her ailing mother, she began working for democratic reforms. She founded the National League for Democracy, bravely spoke out against the military, and called for free elections. "A life of politics holds no attraction for me," she said in August 1988. "At the moment, I serve as a kind of unifying force because of my father's name and because I am not interested in jostling for any kind of position."

As she traveled about the country, people were at first drawn to her because of her striking resemblance to her father—she had the same warm smile, piercing eyes, and direct way of speaking. But it was her message of nonviolent reconciliation that won their support. Courageously, she criticized the military's brutal tactics. In retaliation, the government began arresting her followers and harassing her. On April 5, 1989, an army captain ordered six of his men to shoot Suu Kyi. Just before they fired, a senior officer intervened to prevent her assassination. Three months later,

*Hmong refugees in Thailand. In 1993, there were fourteen million refugees in the world,
most of them indigenous people.*

she was placed under house arrest. She was offered her freedom, but only if she left the country. She chose to stay.

The following spring, Burma's military regime held national elections, and Suu Kyi's democratic party won 392 of 485 parliamentary seats. This was a resounding vote for democracy and peace, but the victory proved hollow. Before they would transfer power to the newly elected officials, the generals insisted that a new constitution be approved by all of the country's one hundred and thirty-five ethnic minorities—an impossible task. The generals knew full well that the only person who could conceivably draw such consensus and cooperation was the woman they were holding under house arrest.

Even in isolation, Suu Kyi inspired her people with her courage and unwavering belief that Burma's disparate cultures can live together.

"It is important in our movement for democracy that all ethnic groups in the country work together," she wrote. "In my youth, I was taught to live closely with people from other ethnic groups. We need to show [them] sympathy and understanding. Without this, progress for the country will be impossible."

In October 1991, the Norwegian Nobel Committee awarded Aung San Suu Kyi the Nobel Peace Prize—"for her unflagging efforts and to show its support for the many people throughout the world who are striving to attain democracy, human rights, and ethnic conciliation by peaceful means."

Suu Kyi remained under house arrest. "I am not sure if the Nobel Peace Prize has ever been given to someone in a situation of such extreme isolation and peril," said her husband. "Suu is now in the third year of her political detention at the hands of Burma's military rulers. We, her family, are denied any contact whatsoever with her and know nothing of her condition except that she is quite alone."

Meanwhile, Burma's military regime has stepped up its attack on the indigenous minorities. Approximately fifteen million Karen, Shan, Karenni, Arakan, and Mon people still live in the mountainous highlands that form Burma's border with Thailand, Laos, and China.

In these remote regions there are no cities or highways, only thousands of small villages, connected by narrow paths that wind through the tropical forest.

The Burmese army has already driven hundreds of thousands of villagers from their homes, crowding them into disease-infested relocation camps. The Karenni government in exile has reported that in March 1992, SLORC ordered twenty thousand people from seventy-six villages into relocation camps. A soldier who defected from the Burmese army and joined the Karenni forces said that his unit had given two villages, with a population totaling thirteen hundred, two days to move. "We burned the houses. We gave the people a location to go to. They took a small amount of food, not enough to live for very long."

The Burmese army has found that to move supplies in the highlands it is cheaper to enslave villagers than to buy pack animals. Since 1988, it has forced tens of thousands of indigenous people to become porters. Some of these are released when they become ill or too weak to shoulder the heavy loads, but in many cases the infirm are shot or simply left to die. Some villagers are sent ahead of the column of troops as human mine detectors: A buried land mine is discovered when it blows away one of their legs.

Women, who are also sometimes forced to haul supplies up the steep slopes, are often raped at night by one or more soldiers. "The soldiers took my husband to be a coolie and then later that same night they came back and raped me," a mother of five in Buthidaung told Amnesty International in 1992. "There were four of them. They took me to their camp and I was kept there all night."

Other casualties of Burma's civil war are the region's once vast hardwood forests. Generations of Karen people have always harvested teak and other hardwoods, but they have taken only mature trees and have always worked with hand saws and elephants, which have considerably less impact on the forest than heavy equipment. The skills of the woodsmen, along with their reverence for the forest as the source of life, were passed from father to son.

But in 1988, Burma sold Thai logging companies the rights to log forty-five large tracts of land belonging to the Karen, Mon, Karenni, and Shan people. Traditional loggers were displaced. The logging roads helped the military advance. Now, with their forests leveled, the indigenous people still left there have little food and no place to hide. And, with terrible irony, Burma has spent money from these sales of logging rights to buy arms used against the indigenous people.

Forty-four years of civil war in Burma have already claimed the lives of half a million indigenous people, most of them humble villagers who lived peacefully in the beautiful forested highlands. "If left unchecked, our forests will be gone forever within the next five years," Dr. Em Marta, a Karen leader, told the United Nations in 1990. "If our forests are gone, the Karen and other indigenous peoples will also fade away."

A Banjara woman, India.

PACIFIC

RESTORING SOVEREIGNTY

*Children in the Bora
Bora lagoon. The
Pacific Ocean covers
one-third of the
surface of the earth
and is home to six
million indigenous
island people—
Melanesians,
Polynesians, and
Micronesians.*

*Children in the Bora
Bora lagoon. The
Pacific Ocean covers
one-third of the
surface of the earth
and is home to six
million indigenous
island people—
Melanesians,
Polynesians, and
Micronesians.*

*Previous page:
A traditional
Tokelauan outrigger
is assembled from
small trees, lashed
with coconut fiber
rope, and caulked
with breadfruit sap.*

On January 16, 1993, Hawaiian governor John Waihee issued an order prohibiting the American flag from being raised that day over the state buildings in Hawaii. Veterans protested. Tourists looked perplexed. Waihee, the state's first governor of Hawaiian ancestry, simply said, "It is important to remember the events of a hundred years ago that stole a nation, and to dedicate ourselves to right that wrong."

On January 16 a hundred years earlier, a contingent of U.S. marines armed with carbines, Gatling guns, and Howitzers landed at Honolulu and marched through the streets to Iolani Palace, the symbolic seat of Hawaii's sovereignty. When Hawaii's Queen Lili'uokalani looked out her window, she saw the guns of the USS *Boston* aimed at the Palace. Lili'uokalani protested that Hawaii was a sovereign nation and that the invasion was a breach of treaty and international law. To avoid bloodshed she surrendered her authority, but only until such time as the United States could review the facts and reinstate the sovereignty of her people.

"Oh, honest Americans," Lili'uokalani pleaded, "as Christians hear me for my down-trodden people! Their form of government is as dear to them as yours is precious to you. Quite as warmly as you love your country, so they love theirs."

Her pleas were ignored by the handful of opportunists who had seized Hawaii, with little more authority than their own avarice and audacity. After convincing the military to threaten the queen into submission, Henry Cooper, an American lawyer who had lived in the islands for less than a year, proclaimed that he and his friends were the "provisional government" of Hawaii. To complete this bizarre coup, they designated Sanford B. Dole, founder of the Dole Fruit Company, as their leader and petitioned the United States to annex Hawaii.

President Grover Cleveland condemned their conspiracy as "an act of war, committed without authority of Congress. The government of a feeble but friendly and confiding people has been overthrown. A substantial wrong has thus been done.

But for the lawless occupation of Honolulu under false pretexts by the United States forces, the Queen would never have yielded. . . . Lili'uokalani knew that she could not withstand the power of the United States, but believed that she might safely trust to its justice."

As long as Cleveland was president, Hawaii's status remained in limbo. But as soon as McKinley came into office, he completed the annexation and appointed his friend Dole to be territorial governor. Dole in turn awarded lucrative government jobs and contracts to his friends, and a coalition of businesses known as "the Big Five" quickly developed regional monopolies in shipping, finance, communications, transportation, and commerce. A dozen men controlled Hawaii's hotels, utilities, banks, sugar industry, and the government itself. A handful of American businessmen had successfully stripped the Hawaiian people of their freedom.

The Hawaiians quickly became a minority in their own land. When Captain James Cook arrived in 1778, a million native people had been living in the islands; by 1893 there were only thirty-five thousand left. With no limits on the number of people who could move to the islands, Native Hawaiians were soon overwhelmed by immigrants preoccupied with making money. By the 1940s, a new generation of native Hawaiians knew little of the illegal overthrow; many did not even know that Hawaii had been an independent nation. In 1959, Hawaiian statehood brought a new wave of economic interests to the islands. Many of the remaining large undeveloped tracts of land were bought by investors from Canada, the United States, Japan, China, and the Arab nations. Developers, builders, and realtors competed in a frenzy of buying, selling, mortgaging, subdividing, and leasing that drove the price of land far beyond the reach of most native Hawaiians.

My friend Jonathan Tolintino, who lives in a small village on Maui, was caught in this bind. While training to become a medical aide, he supported his wife, Pake, and their two daughters by raising papayas. On my visits, Jonathan and I would walk among the trees, using a long pole padded at one end to dislodge the ripe fruit, which could be growing up to twenty feet above the ground. The trick was to hold the prod in one hand and use your other hand to catch the papaya before it landed, all the while making sure no tarantulas had tumbled down with the fruit. Although Jonathan's family had lived in the area for many generations, the only way he could plant an acre or two of papayas was to make an agreement with non-Hawaiian landowners, many of whom lived thousands of miles away and rarely visited their lands.

Some years ago, I spent Christmas with Jonathan and his family, and I remember noticing how their life together embraced the old and the new. At first glance, one might think their family was thoroughly modern. Jonathan was running the health clinic, Pake was coaching junior high volleyball, and their girls were bright, vivacious students who would fit in almost anywhere. But they knew the history of their people and they knew about working hard every day just to get by, while tourists with seemingly endless amounts of cash swarmed over their island. Jonathan's family had every reason to be bitter and antagonistic, but they lived in the old Hawaiian spirit of *Aloha*, sharing and kindness.

One night we stayed up talking, and our conversation eventually turned to the old beliefs and tales of the *acunas*, the ancient Hawaiian priests, who were men of great knowledge and spirit. "Some of the stories from those old days sound strange to our ears," I recall Pake saying. "But when I sit down and really *listen* to our older people, I hear much beauty and wisdom in what they say."

The essence of Hawaiian culture, which people like Jonathan and his family try to live every day, has been battered and discredited in many ways over the years. Poka Laenui, a long-time Hawaiian-rights activist, says, "Our children were forbidden to speak publicly the language of their ancestors. Our children were forced to attend American-run schools. The traditional *hula* was discouraged. The methods of healing with herbs and prayers were ridiculed and labeled 'pagan.' Self-sufficiency was no longer encouraged, and in its place, people were encouraged to work for a wage."

With tourist money flowing into the islands, golf courses, tennis courts, condominiums, and glass towers arose in taro patches and vegetable fields, sometimes obliterating sacred sites. "Meanwhile, many of our people are sleeping in cars or parks hoping to avoid arrest on charges of trespassing," says Laenui. "The most tragic result of this colonization process has been the damage done to the spirit of the people. Our people were once courageous and imaginative, willing to face any challenge. But now we have become docile, believing and fearing that we would be unable to survive if the United States stopped pouring money into Hawaii."

Traditional Hawaiian methods of cultivation and fishing, which once sustained more than a million people, have given way to imported foods. The once sustainable island economy is now hitched to the sugar and pineapple industries, tourism, and military spending. Some of the mountain valleys harbor nuclear weapons. One-fourth of the island of Oahu is occupied by the military. The entire island of Kaho'olawe has been appropriated by the military for training and bombing.

Over time, the loss of lands and language, along with the more subtle pressures of American society, convinced many Hawaiians that their culture was slipping away. "Many of us have accepted captivity and traded our freedom and dignity for a few pieces of silver and citizenship in a nation that has consistently exploited and exposed us to danger and destruction," says Laenui. "Our language, our culture, our religious

A Cook Islander sewing a lei of plumeria blossoms.

practices have been severely damaged. We have only this place, but it's become almost unrecognizable to us. We are like strangers in our own land."

But the people's desire to reclaim their lands and culture has never died out. Beginning in the 1970s, Hawaiians began petitioning the U.S. Congress to address their indigenous rights. Congress responded with such indifference that Hawaiians realized they had to take the initiative. In 1978, they persuaded a state constitutional convention to create the Office of Hawaiian Affairs (OHA), a native Hawaiian entity that would try to regain much of the sovereignty lost in 1893. As a sort of interim government in waiting, OHA has begun the task of reclaiming some lands held in trust for Hawaiians. Under both federal and state jurisdiction, native Hawaiians have received virtually no benefits from their own lands. In

A fresh fruit and vegetable stand in Bora Bora.

fact, most of their lands have been used without payment by the federal government for military bases, nuclear weapons storage, and bombing ranges.

There is now general agreement, among both native and nonnative Hawaiians, that the 1893 overthrow was an illegal and immoral act against a sovereign people and nation. But how are reparations to be made and native Hawaiian sovereignty restored?

The Office of Hawaiian Affairs has proposed a form of indigenous government within the context of the state of Hawaii. If enacted by Congress, a majority of native Hawaiian voters would approve the final framework of sovereignty that would enable them to regulate traditional hunting and fishing, issue land allotments, zone

and manage lands, levy taxes, and administer justice.

"Whether sovereignty works for the Hawaiian people is entirely up to them," says Clayton Hee, Chairman of the Office of Hawaiian Affairs. "And from that point of view it's a good thing. Let us make the decisions we are accountable for, as in the old days before the overthrow. We should have the right to succeed or fail."

Some native Hawaiians decided they couldn't wait for the U.S. Congress to resurrect their nation. In 1978, two hundred and fifty activists wrote their own constitution for the Sovereign Nation of Hawaii. "It is the responsibility of the native people to define sovereignty, to look at models of sovereignty and decide," said Mililani Trask, a native Hawaiian lawyer who became a leader of the new nation. "Our traditional culture will always be the foundation and light of our lives."

One U.S. senator reportedly told her, "You know, Miss Trask, a hundred years ago America overthrew your kingdom. When are you going to realize and accept that fact?" Asked Trask in response, "When are you going to realize that we're not going to vanish, that we've not assimilated and never will?"

This woman, with her dark hair flowing over her shoulders and a voice that moves quickly from anger to warmth, once gave me her card. It read: "Mililani Trask: Governor of the Sovereign Nation of Hawaii." She said, "We have to realize that we are all one small family, native and non-native Hawaiians alike. We need to cross cultural, religious, and racial barriers. We need to work together for ourselves—and because the earth is under assault."

❖

There are islands in the far reaches of the South Pacific that still seem to be beyond this world, beyond the reach of time. Days are measured not by business hours and the changing of traffic lights, but by the rise of trade winds and the turning of tides over coral reefs. Yet every island, however distant and serene, is now vulnerable to the environmental neglect of highly developed countries.

It is no longer just a matter of fishermen finding plastic in their nets and tar balls on their white sand beaches. Oceanic and atmospheric pollution is a day-to-day reality in their lives. Global warming, an academic debate for some, is a matter of life and death for many islanders. The mere possibility of the polar ice caps melting and the sea level rising strikes fear in the hearts of islanders whose homelands barely rise above the sea. If the mean high tide comes up just a foot or two, some islands will be submerged. Time will tell whether global warming causes islands

to disappear, but in the meantime, island people have to live with this fear every day. Stirring their anxiety is their memory of the U.S. government's assertion that the testing of nuclear bombs in their part of the world would be inconsequential for them.

In the 1940s, the United States moved into the remote Marshall Islands, forcibly removed the native people to other islands, and began testing nuclear warheads. In the process, a number of small islands were completely demolished. In 1963, France chose a region near Tahiti where it carried out forty-one nuclear tests. When many non-nuclear countries protested at the United Nations, the French turned to underground testing and detonated more than thirty so-called peaceful explosions.

Although testing has now been curtailed, many Pacific Islanders fear that it is only a matter of time before it is resumed. But regardless of whether another bomb is ever detonated in their region, islanders are haunted by the trauma of past explosions and their release of radiation.

"Our islands are in a dangerous situation," says Tahitian leader Myron Matao. "A couple of our people went underwater after an underground test to look at the Mururoa atoll. They discovered cracks appearing in the ocean floor. This island is sinking. And I believe that, as it sinks, the accumulated radiation will get free and poison our entire environment."

Matao maintains that cancer, previously rare among his people, is now reaching epidemic proportions. "Out of 1,093 people who died in a three-year period, 70 died because of cancer. That's much too many. An uncle of mine died from it. He lived on an atoll about a hundred miles from Mururoa. Cancer had never existed on that island before. I'm sure he was contaminated because of the atomic tests. Polynesians eat a lot of fish. Every day my uncle ate fish. Around Mururoa you can no longer eat anything that comes from the land or the sea. It's not only our people who are endangered. Many species of fish from our territory travel great distances. Radioactive turtles have been caught in Peru. So what should we do? We can only fight with words. But words are sometimes too weak."

The clash of traditional and modern values is intensifying throughout the Pacific. In some instances, alternatives are clearly drawn. Should an island nation such as Fiji, for example, continue building resort hotels that are profitable but beyond the reach of most Fijians to own or manage? Or should the island's limited land be used to develop small-scale market farming to satisfy local needs?

The outside world's advertisements, consumer goods, television shows, movies, magazines, and ubiquitous flocks of tourists all convey the message that the highly consumptive Western way of life is the good life. But those who cannot afford the glittering products and technology often find their sense of self-worth slipping away. Everything carries a price, and some islanders are beginning to question the need to catch up with more developed societies by importing their technology, culture, institutions, and ways of solving community problems.

Success in the modern world, reflects Jane Dakuvulu of Fiji, "is attainable only at the cost of sacrificing other values we cherish: the warmth and strength of our extended family relationships, the respect we have for our elders and chiefs, our freer attitude about time. If we do not want to sacrifice too many of our old values on the altar of modernization, then we should be more careful about equating quality with quantity, of pricing people's worth according to their possessions."

This basic conflict arises in one island nation after another. The Solomon Islanders, who live due east of Papua New Guinea and have been independent from Britain since 1978, are one of many island cultures in transition between traditional and modern ways of living. There are three hundred thousand Solomon Islanders,

and like all peoples, they want to survive— and in their own way.

"I feel our problems can only be tackled from within," says Francis Gugotu, a leader of the Solomon Islanders. "The problems of the oppressed must be solved by the oppressed, who first of all must accept their position as such and then transform it. One essential way of recapturing pride and identity will be for Solomon Islanders to see the hollowness of Western-style 'progress.' Solomon Islanders need to look at themselves and the past not merely for symbols, but for strengths their colonizers have lost, for wisdom and values people everywhere seem to be seeking right now."

While the economic consequences of colonialism are usually all too apparent, the psychological effects often slip silently, in disguise, into people's lives. Whether the colonizer is a nation-state or a multinational corporation, simply by enticing the indigenous peoples to adopt new values and a new way of life, it can foster attitudes of compliance and subservience. As Gugotu puts it, "We must have faith in ourselves and our cultures." He suggests that one way to look past "the new darkness brought about by the dazzling lights of civilization" is to reaffirm the strengths of the traditional way of life. Communal land rights, which in years past helped define the community and draw people together, could replace private ownership, at least in some areas. Collective responsibility could form the basis for cooperative work in business ventures and community development projects. This might extend to shared responsibility for the young, the sick, and the elderly, which could replace dependence on the welfare system.

In many instances, reestablishing traditional values begins with a careful look at the technologies that changed the traditional ways of doing things. Any new technology carries a social value and, often, unexpected consequences. Something as seemingly innocuous as a refrigerator can change values and relationships within a community. In the past, twenty or so islanders would go out fishing, and the two or three who had good luck would share their catch. People helped each other. No one ate while others went hungry. But as soon as the first refrigerator arrived, its owner could store away the catch for another day. Pretty soon everyone would have to have a refrigerator, and the custom of sharing the day's catch would be lost. And when some villagers could afford refrigerators and others could not, a sense of rich-versus-poor would creep in. Then, with the villagers dependent upon the new technology, the community would have to find the funds to generate more electricity. In this way would the chain of social upheavals that started with that first refrigerator go on and on.

How does an individual or community extricate itself from such cycles of cultural alienation? The first step is deciding one wants to. And then begins the process of examining the consequences of development, *all* its consequences. For indigenous peoples of the South Pacific and elsewhere, development is closely linked with the desire for freedom. Material possessions are far less important than the freedom to live a fulfilling life. In the Solomon Islands, some native people are drawn to a more urban, cash-oriented lifestyle. But the majority still express the wish to remain *themselves* and to evolve a new Solomon Island way by refining and giving new meaning to traditional village life.

The challenge for Pacific Islanders, says Gugotu, "is not to stand wide-eyed at one side of the arena, blankly watching our interests being manipulated by foreigners, but to stand in the center of the ring and be involved."

Children of the nuclear age. The United States, Britain, and France have detonated more than two hundred nuclear bombs in the South Pacific.

IGOROT

INDIGENOUS WAR IN THE PHILIPPINES

O n the morning of April 24, 1992, I found myself squeezed into a jeep that swerved and jolted up a narrow mountain road in the Philippine Cordillera. The Cordillera People's Alliance (CPA), a federation of indigenous organizations, had invited me to a Cordillera Day gathering. For more than an hour after leaving Baguio City, we bounced along a one-lane dirt road, passing clusters of patchwork wood and tin houses. Chickens, pigs, and children scurried away at the sound of our horn. The road ended abruptly at the base of a mountain. An indigenous woman checked our identification, and we joined others hiking up a rocky switchback trail to the mountaintop, where several thousand Igorots were already camped.

For these indigenous people, Cordillera Day was not so much a celebration as a time of unity and solidarity in memory of their beloved Macliing Dulag. Twelve years before, Dulag had organized opposition to the Marcos government's plans to build a series of hydroelectric dams on the Chico River that would submerge entire villages and render more than eighty-five thousand of his people homeless. Dulag, a highly respected elder and father of six, pleaded with the government not to build the dams.

The government told Dulag that the Igorot people had no title to the land. Dulag said their ownership came down from their ancestors. You'll have to move, said the government. "We won't," said Dulag. "You ask if we own the land and mock us, saying, 'Where is your title?' Such arrogance, to speak of owning the land when we are instead owned by it. How can you own that which will outlive you? Land is a grace that must be nurtured. Land is sacred and beloved."

For months Dulag traveled up and down the Chico, urging villagers to resist. Then, on April 24, 1980, a small band of government soldiers came to his village of Bugnay looking for him. His wife recalls that she and Macliing were awakened that night by loud knocking at the side door. While Macliing was putting on his clothes, the door latch gave way to the pounding of rifle butts. As he reached for the latch, bullets burst through the door, hitting him in the chest. He died instantly.

This man is one of six and a half million indigenous people of more than fifty distinct cultures in the Philippines.

Dulag's death galvanized opposition to the dams. Protests increased. Dam-building equipment was vandalized. And violence erupted.

"The killings that are going on in Kalinga in the aftermath of Macliing Dulag's murder will not come to an end until all work on the Chico River dams is brought to a complete stop." So wrote the Bishop of Malaybalay to Philippine President Ferdinand Marcos. "The government must effectively show the people that it does not want to exterminate them."

The soldier who shot Macliing Dulag was eventually brought to trial and convicted. His punishment? Transfer to another region. Hostilities surrounding the Chico River dams continued until construction workers walked off the job to protect their own safety. The Cordillera people believe that they will return if the military subdues their region.

❖

In memory of Dulag's courage, the Igorots observe April 24 as Cordillera Day. With at least four thousand people camped on the mountaintop, the 1992 gathering was the largest ever. As I mingled with the various groups of people, I began to realize that I was the only American present. Everyone was friendly toward me, but the strong anti-U.S. sentiment was hard to miss.

"You might think we would be happy to have U.S. military bases in our country," said Minnie Degawan, the CPA's energetic director of international programs. "Yes, the bases bring lots of money into the Philippines, but they represent the repression we are trying to overcome. We need elections free of military threat. We need to free ourselves of feeling controlled and intimidated. And we need to be free of our huge national debt. It's already more than $35 billion, most of it owed to the U.S. To reduce the debt, the government wants to strip resources from the Cordillera. When we object, government soldiers, backed by the U.S., try to repress us. It's as if we were still a colony."

Minnie explained that many of her country's current problems are rooted in its colonial past. When the Spanish arrived in 1565, the Philippines was not a country with a national identity, but rather comprised hundreds of territories held by tribal groups, who traded and warred with each other. Under colonial rule, traditional beliefs gave way to Catholicism, and the Spanish cut the lowland forests and planted them in sugar cane, took gold from the hills, and levied taxes.

While some Filipinos began assimilating and working with the Spanish, others resisted, and none more fiercely than the five indigenous peoples in the Cordillera known collectively as the Igorots. Spaniards burned Igorot houses and crops, raped the women, and tried to take the lands. But during three hundred and fifty years of Spanish occupation, the Igorots never surrendered.

Meanwhile, in the lowlands, a class of wealthy Filipinos was emerging, collaborating with the Spanish in exploiting both the land and poorer people. In 1900, when U.S. occupation began, the Filipino elite quickly switched its allegiance from the Spanish to the Americans. It thus earned preferential access to Philippine resources and American markets and grew very rich. On July 4, 1946, the U.S. granted independence to the Republic of the Philippines, but the country was hardly free. As one U.S. military analyst acknowledged, "In spite of their independence, the Philippines are of course extremely dependent on us militarily, economically, and politically. At the moment, their independence consists principally of face."

To this day, Filipinos are striving for independence from economic repression and for a truly democratic government. Consequently, the struggle of the Igorots and other indigenous Filipinos has taken on a different character from those of native peoples elsewhere in the world. In addition to fighting for their rights as distinct peoples, they have united with nonindigenous people in the effort to make democracy work.

An Igorot family works their rice field in the Philippine Cordillera.

As Cordillera Day progressed, groups of villagers took turns singing, and circles of dancers moved gracefully to the reverberating tones of Igorot gongs. But for all the joy of the music and dancing, there was also a serious task at hand. The villagers had not come to this mountaintop for its sweeping views, but because, for at least this one day, it was a safe place to talk.

"Fifty families have been evacuated from our village," said an old woman from the Mountain Province, where government forces were engaged in a prolonged struggle with the insurgent New People's Army (NPA), formed in the early 1960s to counter the repressive actions of Ferdinand Marcos. "Nine days ago there was a gun battle—we didn't know if we'd be killed by the military or the NPA."

"When our people have tried to return to their homes, they've been shot and drowned in the river," said a man from the Marag Valley on the north coast. "Our people want to go home. There are a few of them left in the Marag Valley, but they are hiding in the forest."

An older, plainly dressed woman walked up to me. "In my village near Sagada, eight soldiers raped a woman," she whispered in slow but clear English. "The woman was married and managed to get home to her husband. She told him what happened and then died. He had been a gentle person, but the thought of all those soldiers raping his wife enraged him. He joined the NPA and became known for his daring attacks on the military."

I met three refugees whom the Cordillera People's Alliance had been protecting in Baguio City. Six months earlier, soldiers had threatened to rape their wives if they refused to join a paramilitary unit. They were accused of being sympathetic to the New People's Army.

"We just wanted to defend our culture,

and for that they threatened to kill us," said one of the refugees. "We are fighting not just for our lives, but for our land and the future of our people. We know that the military coming in here is just the beginning. If they control us, they'll come back to build the dams and our village will disappear."

Throughout the day, reports came in from all over the Cordillera. Hit-and-run attacks on villagers by soldiers, rebels, and an assortment of paramilitary units were tearing the Cordillera apart. The NPA was fighting back. The government called this state of violence a rebel insurgency. People in the Cordillera called it a total war.

One area around the village of Conner remained something of a black hole, from which virtually no information emerged. The previous year, the military had assassinated the CPA's staff person in Conner. Now there were rumors of rapes, bombings, and burned houses, but no substantiated reports, no hard facts. At the conclusion of Cordillera Day, a fact-finding mission was formed, and the government granted it tentative permission to enter the region. A medical team would follow in a week.

I was invited to join the mission to Conner, with the warning that the military might not allow an American to go in. And if it did, I'd have to keep my eyes open for the NPA, which was already holding one American hostage. We drove north from Baguio through Tuguegarao's dusty streets, bustling with pony carts and motorized tricycles, and passed through a series of military checkpoints. Then we reached the final roadblock, an encampment of soldiers with a row of American-made troop-transport trucks, their names painted in bold letters: ULTIMATE WARRIOR, TEXAS TORNADO, BUSHWHACKER, LEGION OF DOOM.

The soldiers milled around with their machine guns held waist high. One of them checked our identification. I was asked to step aside.

"You're an American?" the guard asked. "Why do you want to come in here?"

"Well, I'm interested in native cultures, and this seems like a good opportunity to meet some village people. I'd like to compare their lives to native people in Alaska," I said, trying my best to sound like an earnest anthropology student.

"I'm afraid this place isn't for you."

"Why not?"

"Don't you know there's a war going on? The NPA is all over the place. We can't protect you."

❖

Instead of going to Conner, I spent the day driving to Pamplona on the north coast with Father Mike, an expatriate American priest who has made the Philippines his home for thirty years. Once, in his own church, someone shot him in the leg.

"These people are very warm and friendly," Father Mike told me. "But they can also be very cruel. Opposites come close together."

By chance, our arrival in Pamplona coincided with a visit by General Robert Manlongot, who was trying to enlist the archbishop's assistance in negotiating with the NPA rebels. In a fresh polo shirt and casual slacks, Manlongot looked as if he had just strolled off the country club's back nine. I had to remind myself that this affable, boyish-looking man was the one they called the "Tiger of Marag," the only field commander able to take the Marag Valley. His troops were "credited" with burning eighty-eight homes. Three hundred families were now living as refugees in the forest. Manlongot's new assignment was the Cordillera.

"When I came here, I moved in slowly, setting up camps," Manlongot told me. "I studied the situation before making my plan."

"What kind of plan?" I asked. His eyes twinkled.

"I see this as a people's war, so you have to fight it as a people's war," he said. "You know, involve people. Get the clergy in there, and civilians. Provide a little development as well as fighting the NPA."

"What do you think the NPA wants from this civil war?" I asked.

"This is not a civil war!" he shot back. "This is just an insurgency. And to fight it, I give the village people a little something. I come in and hire local people to help build an elementary school. People begin to see that we are their friends."

"Aren't some village people friends of the NPA?" I asked.

"Of course. When men appear with guns, what are you going to do? You feed them."

"So, who is going to win? You or the NPA?"

"We will, of course. The Philippines cannot tolerate the NPA or any other army in our country. We will talk them into surrendering or we'll blast them out any way we have to."

"What about making the land reforms they seek?" I asked. "I sense it's important to these people to own the land their ancestors worked."

"Land reform. Land reform. The NPA doesn't really understand what land reform is. You can't come up with one blanket reform and throw it over the whole country. The nuts and bolts of land reform are going to be different in every province."

Accompanying the general was the only American I saw during my three weeks in the Cordillera. He was a quiet, fastidiously neat U.S. official who was seeking the release of the American being held hostage by the NPA.

"Do you think it's safe for me to meet with any of these rebel soldiers?" I asked, as nonchalantly as I could.

"Oh, they'll love you," said a Filipino woman, before the official responded. "You're an American," she laughed. "The rebels will figure they can get a lot of money if they kidnap you. Even a few thousand dollars is a fortune to them."

Maybe she was just kidding, I told myself. But that night I decided I'd try to avoid the NPA. In the morning the Conner mission returned with a grim report. The villagers had endured daily bombings. Young girls had been raped. Men were missing. On Cordillera Day itself, the military had burned a village to the ground. I was stunned by photos of people sifting through the charred remains of their homes, looking for a pot or tool, for anything that might still be useful. When I was invited on a fact-finding mission to Tanlag, where the rebels and military were fighting, I said I'd go.

The next day, I joined five others on a trip to Tanlag in an ornately decorated jeepney, one of those dusty, open-air minivans with bench seats that are popular in Southeast Asia. The three-hour ride from Tabuk took us past rice fields being worked by peasants and their water buffalo, then up through broad, grass-covered hills, and finally into the precipitous canyon of the Chico, where our driver delighted in sliding around blind corners, turning up dust and gravel. From this ridgetop road, one normally reaches Tanlag by hiking down several thousand feet, swimming the Chico River, and then climbing up the far bank. But these were not normal times, and for us, getting to Tanlag would be a little trickier. Government soldiers held the road. Rebel fighters were somewhere out in the woods. The villagers were caught in between.

To avoid the military, we crossed the Chico River several miles downstream and slowly worked our way along a seldom used trail to Tanlag. In places, landslides had obliterated the narrow path, and we had to edge along the cliff, holding onto bamboo shoots.

After hiking through the heat for most of the day, we rounded a bend, and there before us lay the lush, light-green rice terraces of Tanlag. In the village, I was overcome by two conflicting feelings. On the one hand, I felt that I had walked into a corner of the world that had been bypassed by the commotion of the twentieth century. With no road or cars, radios or television, the village had an unusual serenity. Children laughed as they played games on the dusty pathways. A teenager strummed his guitar while friends sang local ballads and songs like "Let It Be" and "A Bridge Over Troubled Waters."

But the serenity was laced with a fear that seemed to grip each of the three hundred people who lived here. A woman told me she was afraid to work in the fields. A man said that if he hiked up to the road, he might be shot by soldiers. I was shown the grave of a man who had been killed for speaking up on behalf of the village.

An eighty-year-old man and his wife invited me into their home. Just two weeks before, they had been awakened early in the morning by the sounds of gunshots. Bullets had ripped through the walls of their small house. They had survived the attack by hiding among their hogs.

"This is a very poor place. We are all threatened here," said the old man. "We have no road, no communication with the rest of the world."

"Can't you ask the government for help?" I asked.

"When one of our village leaders spoke out, the government shot him," he answered. "My wife and I are old now, but we still want to live. Please don't tell anyone my name—if they find out I talked with you, they will come and kill me."

The old man spoke in his native dialect and his words were translated by Tina Dumalyong, a young woman in her early twenties. She had a quick smile that lit up her face, but there was anxiety in her eyes.

"Are you ever afraid?" I asked her.

"Actually, I'm afraid even now," she said. "Whenever the soldiers are around, anything can happen. Before, we could go anywhere we wanted. Now we are afraid to work in the rice fields because soldiers could come. But if we can't go to the fields we will all go hungry."

"Who do the people here see as their enemy?" I asked. "The NPA or the government soldiers?"

"In Tanlag, our number one hope is that the military will go home," she said. "We have no means to fight against them. The more we protest, the more we are tortured. So we try to keep calm, just keep quiet. Nobody hears our sorrow, our grief."

At that moment, a man I'd noticed watching me earlier approached and motioned me to follow him. When we were out of hearing of the others, he whispered, "There is an NPA soldier in the village. He wants to talk with you."

As he led me along a twisting pathway, I noticed my heart beating a little faster. "Relax, Art," I told myself, "just take a deep breath." At the far side of the village, we slipped into a small, darkened home. A man who appeared to be in his late twenties rose as we entered. He was lean, his face gaunt. My guide left, and I was alone with the rebel soldier.

"I apologize for my poor English," he said, breaking a moment of awkward silence.

"Well, I'm afraid I don't speak a word of your language," I said.

As we began talking, I found his pleasant, somewhat shy manner disarming. I had to remind myself that at this very moment some of his compatriots were holding an American hostage. The man I faced had a machine gun close at hand and a long knife hung from his belt. We both knew that he could easily take me hostage.

"How did you come to join the New People's Army?" I asked.

"As a student, I was an activist for six years. After I got my engineering degree, I got a job, but I still tried to work for social change. We need many things. But the government is deaf to the needs of the people. There is no real democracy in the Philippines. Both politics and the economy are controlled by a few wealthy people. So I finally joined the NPA, to fight for the essence of democracy."

"What do you mean, 'the essence of democracy'?"

"A chance to determine our future. A chance to voice our beliefs without fear of being killed. And we want our country's resources to benefit Filipinos. I don't know if the average American realizes it, but American corporations are taking away our country's resources—timber, minerals, everything of value. And the U.S. sends back military aide. Who is it used against? Not other countries. All the guns, armored cars, and planes are used against Philippine people, the poor people, like the ones you see here in Tanlag."

"So, how does this make you feel about Americans?" I asked, trying to contain my nervousness.

"Don't worry," he said, smiling. "I don't hate you because you are an American. We don't view American people as our enemies, only those in government or business who want to control or exploit us."

"Are you ever afraid?" I asked him.

"I used to be. But not anymore. You see, before joining the NPA all of us had to reach that point where we are ready to die for our beliefs. As part of our initiation we pledge: 'I will die for the benefit of the people and to achieve democracy.' So I have already accepted that I might be killed."

"Do you have children?"

"No, but someday I hope to. To go underground you must sacrifice everything. Leave your family. Sometimes it's very difficult for me. But I have hope . . ."

His voice trailed off. He looked down at the floor for what seemed like several minutes, then he looked up and past me. As if talking to someone else, he said, "I have to have hope that someday we will be free."

An Igorot woman of the Ifugao tribe in the Philippine Cordillera.

INDONESIA

THE POLITICS OF GENOCIDE

*T*he Great Escape. Bali and Indonesia have something to suit every traveler. Play tennis, take a dip in one of the pools, or sit back and enjoy the Balinese Cultural Night at the moonlit open-air stage," reads a travel brochure. "Cruise remote waters to the fabled Spice Islands," suggests another tour operator, who promises to "take passengers to the island of Timor, calling on villagers who rarely see visitors."

But beyond the Spice Island romance lies another Indonesia.

"We feel despair," says one village woman of the government's actions against her people. "They have ruined the land and everything on it, the ancient forest which was so vast. For us older people, our time is already up. But we have to think of our children and grandchildren—where are they going to find food? Where are they going to live?"

A tour of Indonesia's Siberut Island offers tourists a chance to visit "primitive tribal people with tattoos, wearing loincloths." But the Siberut people are forbidden to wear their loincloths unless tourists are around. As for a "pampered" tour of East Timor, a Catholic priest writes, in a letter smuggled from this island, that "a barbarous genocide of innocent people goes on. The Timorese did not attack Indonesia. But now Timor is being wiped out by an invasion, a brutal conquest that produces heaps of dead, maimed, and orphaned."

❖

A tribesman of New Guinea, which harbors nearly a thousand distinct cultures and their languages—roughly one-fifth of the world's total of both.

To understand Indonesia's long-running battle with its indigenous peoples, it helps to look back to how this nation emerged from the aftermath of World War II. On August 17, 1945, President Sukarno proclaimed Indonesia's independence and sought control of the far-flung reaches of the former Dutch East Indies. A top aide warned that trying to control such culturally diverse peoples "is not going to work. They are totally different people, totally different cultures. We should have nothing to do with them."

But Sukarno was determined to forge these hundreds of distinct cultures into a nation. He ensconced his government in Djakarta on the island of Java, and ruled with an iron hand and an eye to expansion. One of his first targets was New Guinea, the most culturally diverse place on earth. This one island harbors nearly a thousand distinct languages and cultures—one-fifth of the world's total.

Not until the 1930s did the Europeans venture into its mountainous interior. They went looking for gold, and unexpectedly discovered a lost world—millions of tribal people living a Stone Age life in the twentieth century. They appear to have been there for fifty thousand years, growing crops long before the first attempts at cultivation were made in Mesopotamia.

But it was not ancient cultures Sukarno had in mind when he went after New Guinea; he saw an island covered with hardwood forests, its highlands rich with minerals. He soon focused in on the Dutch-controlled western half of New Guinea know as West Papua. In 1962, he went to the United Nations to engineer the so-called New York agreement: In six years West Papuans would decide whether they wanted to become an independent nation. However, a few months after signing the agreement, Sukarno took matters into his own hands. With the United States pressuring the Dutch and the United Nations looking the other way, he occupied West Papua and renamed it Irian Jaya. The profit-driven regime in Djakarta had taken control of the world's most extraordinary fount of cultural and biological diversity.

No one is sure just how many species of birds, insects, reptiles, flowers, and herbs have evolved in the dense jungles and highland forests of New Guinea. Here, too, live seven hundred thousand West Papuans, who belong to some two hundred and sixty tribes speaking as many languages. The people of each group are unique, following their own evolutionary paths and maintaining distinctive cultures. But the West Papuans are caught in currents of change that they are just beginning to understand, and the things they hold most dear and sacred are drifting away.

It is said that one West Papuan tribe remains unknown, hidden from civilization. Missionaries have set gifts of mirrors, fabrics, and tools at the edges of their territories to coax these people from the forest. But the clergy return to find their offerings trampled and strewn about the ground. Some say that these elusive tribespeople believe that if they accept enticements from civilization, their spirit will leave them and they will be lost.

Whether this aversion to the modern world arises from some mythic impulse or from simply observing the fate of other tribes, it has helped prolong one group's protective isolation. But the stay of cultural execution is only temporary. If Indonesian policies are not changed, virtually all of West Papua's tribal people will be culturally extinct within fifty years.

The fate of the Moi, who live on the western tip of the island and now number about four thousand, is in essence the fate of the Dani, the Asmat, and all the rest of the West Papuan peoples. "Tearing down our forest is like tearing out our hearts," said one Moi tribesman as loggers began leveling the forest near his village.

"All the streams have dried up or become muddy," said another. "The fish we used to catch have disappeared. The water is not clear anymore. And the birds of paradise have also disappeared; they have flown away to other places."

The Moi are forest dwellers who fish for freshwater shrimp, hunt kangaroo and wild pigs, catch birds, and gather greens, fruits, and the nutritious sago palm. They are totally dependent on the forest. But with the government's sanctions, the Intimpura logging company is cutting eight hundred and thirty-seven thousand acres of trees in the heart of Moi ancestral lands. Areas being logged are usually closed to outside visitors, but

A Dani woman. "We feel despair because they have ruined the ancient forest which was so vast. There are no fish, there are no birds, there is nothing left at all."

in January 1992, Ian MacKenzie of the Canadian-based Endangered Peoples Project managed to slip into the Moi region. He found that in addition to cutting trees, Intimpura was carelessly building roads over streams. Said MacKenzie, "Perhaps the greatest danger lies in the very existence of the roads. They will permit the entry of more loggers, both legal and illegal, poachers, and settlers. If the logging is not halted, the Moi are likely to disappear within ten years."

The Moi have virtually no way of defending themselves against this onslaught of loggers, roads, and settlers. Moi lands are "owned" by clans and communities, not by individuals, but Indonesia refuses to recognize their land rights. "They treat us, the owners of the land, as if we

were nobodies," one villager told a visitor when there were no soldiers nearby. "They treat us as if we were worthless people, people with no rights. But we *are* the people who have a right to this land, an absolute right. Why then have they come and ripped everything apart?"

To make such protests openly is to court disaster. The Indonesian army is directed to "assist in the national development," and those who oppose national development can be found guilty of subversion. The military routinely arrests or assassinates those who dare to stand in its way. To this day, tribal men armed with bows, arrows, and the courage of desperation do battle with soldiers toting M-16s.

Nobody knows how many tens, or perhaps hundreds, of thousands of indigenous people have died in the massacres. Indonesia has managed to keep this kind of information from the outside world. After Ian MacKenzie reported the impact of large-scale logging in West Papua, the government added his name to a growing list of journalists prohibited from entering the country. And in 1992, a Swedish filmmaker documenting human rights abuses in West Papua was found on a trail with his throat slit. His wallet was undisturbed, but his videotapes were missing. Said MacKenzie, "The government was sending a message to anyone thinking about telling the world what is happening to the indigenous peoples."

In this well-orchestrated climate of fear, both the atrocities and the determination of the West Papuans tend to go unreported and unnoticed.

"Others may laugh at our customs and how we are so closely related to the land and all things that grow on the land," a West Papuan elder told the young people of his tribe. "But all the trees, animals, fish, insects, reptiles, and even mountains have special meaning for us. Long before the whites came here, these things were very sacred, because they were part of our well-being. For many years we have lived a good and

A West Papuan tribesman. "The Indonesians are trying their best to eliminate our tribal people," says West Papuan activist Viktor Kaisiepo. "We're trying hard to protect everything that is indigenous to us."

happy life, as our ancestors lived before us. We worked together, feasted together, and had our own form of tribal government. But we can no longer live a good communal life. I am sorry, very sorry, to say that you may lose your ancestral lands to land-hungry governments. You will realize that you have lost almost everything that goes with the land. As an old man who is ready for dying, I would like to say, my children, whatever you do, never, and I repeat never, lose your traditional rights over your ancestral lands."

❖

If Indonesia's assault on its land and people is to be halted before the forests and forest people are gone, help must come from outside the country. One man who has dedicated his life

to this effort is Viktor Kaisiepo, a West Papuan living in exile in the Netherlands.

In May 1992, I met Viktor at Kari-Oca, Brazil, the large open-air compound on the outskirts of Rio de Janiero where about five hundred native leaders gathered for the first World Conference of Indigenous Peoples. My first sight of this man caught my interest: dark-skinned with thick curly hair and a beard, he was wearing a bright red shirt and waving his arms and hands as he talked. Viktor had been chosen to lead the English-speaking group, and was very gregarious, turning from one person to another, drawing everyone out, serious one moment, full of jokes the next. Once the meetings wound down, Viktor and I had a chance to talk about his hopes for the people of West Papua.

"My political work is now the most important thing in my life," Viktor told me. "I quit my job solely to do this work. I don't mind losing my pension. I might be dead tomorrow, so to hell with the pension. The reason I'm here in Brazil is to see whether we are alone or if other indigenous peoples face the same problems we do in West Papua. And they do. So we need to come up with a common strategy for survival. It's no use solving the problem in one spot while ignoring the pattern of exploitation worldwide."

Viktor was following in the footsteps of his father, a tribal leader who had fought all his life for West Papuan independence. Their family had been forced to live in exile in the Netherlands from the time Viktor was fourteen. For nearly twenty years Viktor juggled his efforts for West Papua with his career as a sales representative. At thirty-five, he made a choice between his own prosperity and his people's independence. "I chose for my people, though I don't earn a penny from it.

"My people were pirates. We fought the Portuguese. We fought the Spanish and the Dutch. We sailed about, traded, and fought whenever we had to. So we got used to dealing with the outside world. In a confrontation, some people pull back, but we go for it. That's our attitude. I'm nuts over my tribe. But I am West Papuan first, and I'm fighting for the independence of all the tribal groups."

However, the West Papuans' long-sought independence may be undercut by one of the most insidious and least understood strategies being directed at indigenous peoples—transmigration, the government's program of sending in people from other regions to settle in remote ancestral homelands. In West Papua, transmigration supplies cheap immigrant labor for the logging operators, but its hidden agenda is to extend government control over indigenous peoples. Taking a lesson from history, Indonesia knows that if it erases cultural identities, a potential source of racial tension will be eliminated. "The different ethnic groups," says Indonesia's minister of transmigration, "will in the long run disappear because of integration, and there will be one kind of man."

"Thousands of families are being sent to West Papua," Viktor told me. "The first thing they need is land. But all the land is our traditional land. We cannot sell it. We can't live without it. But the Indonesian government is tricky. It tells the world that, yes, the land belongs to indigenous peoples. Sounds good. But the land belongs to us only until the government needs it. Then it belongs to the state. This means we have no rights whatsoever. If the government wants your land, you have to move. Just like that."

As part of its systematic attempt to eliminate its indigenous peoples, Indonesia has prohibited the drawing of all racial distinctions. "It's forbidden for me and my countrymen to address each other as Papuans," said Viktor. "It's forbidden because we'd be referring to our own cultural identity, and that's illegal."

"Are some West Papuans going along with this?"

"No. No way. Probably 99.9 percent don't

go along. And this clash of cultures is at the root of most of the problems we face today. According to the Indonesians, West Papuans who are Melanesians are primitive and backward. The mostly Muslim Indonesians are extremely prejudiced. This is an apartheid system. People condemn apartheid when it's white against black, but not when it's yellow or black against black. But why is that? Discrimination is discrimination!"

As part of the drive for independence, Viktor publishes a bimonthly magazine called *Suara Papua: Voice of the West Papuans*, and smuggles copies into West Papua. He told me, "We tell our people, 'Don't blame the Indonesian migrant or Japanese tourist for our miserable situation. It's the Indonesian government that's exploiting us. And it's the World Bank and the northern industrialized nations that have enormous development interests in our country.'"

"It must feel overwhelming at times."

"Yes, but we have to risk speaking out. Sometimes we are isolated by fear. A person can be jailed, tortured, even killed for being found with a copy of our magazine. I once got a letter from a man in jail who said, 'Could you please send me the magazine?' He was jailed for raising the West Papuan flag. Twenty years. I couldn't do as he asked because it might have finished him."

"Twenty years for hoisting a flag?" I asked, amazed.

"Twenty years. The government called it a matter of national interest. They recently passed a law making any kind of protest punishable as an act of subversion."

"But such persecution helps to unify your people."

"Those of us who live in exile represent the diplomatic and political arm of our movement to free our people. I can't go back. I'd be shot if I did. But we are not only fighting the military within the country. We have come to realize that all the industrialized countries of the North are also hurting us.

"Look at the Freeport mining company, for example. It's a multinational corporation from the United States. It started operating in West Papua in 1967. The company was afraid that Papuan independence would create instability that might disrupt its digging for copper. So it used its influence with the government to help prevent our independence. And Freeport has taken billions of resource dollars from our country. None of it trickles back to the local people."

In the process of taking twenty-five million tons of copper from West Papua, Freeport excavated an enormous open-pit mine on the traditional lands of the Amungme people. A mountain once held sacred has been leveled, the people have lost their livelihood, and effluents from the mine have polluted waters downstream.

"We know the mining and logging companies don't care about us or about democratic principles, but you'd think the American people still would," said Viktor. "We have looked upon the United States as the heart of democracy, but we don't know if Americans stand up for their principles anymore. Watching the U.S. be a silent partner in putting down our independence and destroying our forests and people is the biggest disillusionment we have experienced.

"But I don't want to exclude the Japanese," continued Viktor. "After finishing off the forests of Borneo, they have moved into West Papua to cut the mangrove forests along the coast. The Marubeni Company is chopping trees into wood chips. They take everything. None of these corporations gives anything back to the people. And the Indonesian government helps them steal our country, piece by piece. Japan and the United States never object."

"It must seem like no one gives a damn about what is happening to you."

"That is true. And you see, it's not just my tribe or just the West Papuans fighting for our human rights. It's all the indigenous peoples of Indonesia. We need the support of the United States. Our indigenous cultures won't last much longer. No way, no way. So I feel sorry, and that's what I'm trying . . ."

Viktor's voice trailed off. For a moment, he was unable to speak. Then he said, "I try to tell our people, 'Look, we must keep fighting for our independence. Many nations fall apart. Where is the Soviet Union now? Where is Yugoslavia? Pretty soon it will be Indonesia. It may take ten years, or thirty. So don't feel lost. We can't lose hope.'"

❖

Indonesia's treatment of the Maubere people of East Timor gives another indication of just how long and tortuous West Papua's road to freedom may be.

The Maubere are not an isolated culture, suddenly thrust into the twentieth century, but survivors of three hundred and fifty years of Portuguese colonization. They subsist mainly by cultivating rice, maize, and root crops, and by raising buffalos, pigs, and goats.

When the Portuguese pulled out of East Timor in 1975, the Maubere experienced a one-week interlude of independence. The left-leaning coalition had barely settled into office when Indonesia struck. To gain control, the Indonesian army launched an attack that may become known as this century's most devastating assault on indigenous people.

Just twelve hours before this invasion of East Timor began, U.S. President Gerald Ford arrived in Indonesia. Officially, his visit was said to have no connection with the impending attack. Ford was accompanied by Secretary of State Henry Kissinger, who warned the U.S. ambassador to Indonesia not to discuss Timor "on the grounds that the United States is involved in enough problems of greater importance at present."

In turn, the U.S. ambassador told colleagues that the United States hoped Indonesia would complete its invasion "effectively, quickly, and not use our equipment."

However, U.S. weapons were used from the beginning, and bombing by American-built counterinsurgency aircraft wreaked havoc on villages and crops. At the time, U.S. officials maintained that the use of American weapons for offensive purposes, which would have been a violation of U.S. law, did not occur. Later, George Aldrich, a legal advisor to the State Department, conceded that the Indonesians "were armed roughly 90 percent with our equipment."

The Indonesians found themselves conducting a prolonged war. Through 1976, they injured or killed thousands of East Timorese people in bombing raids. Next, they deliberately destroyed food crops, and in the ensuing famine thousands more East Timorese starved. The survivors had to leave their villages, many fleeing to the hills, where they held out against the Indonesian army until 1978. In that year, the Indonesian army mounted a massive ground and air assault, using chemical weapons and napalm. Stricken by malnutrition and disease, many Maubere people surrendered and were sent to "settlement camps."

"If you go to the camps, things are completely hopeless," a witness reported to Amnesty International. "The procedure was to interrogate the captives or those who had surrendered. During the interrogations they were normally tortured . . . by hitting them with a blunt instrument, by jabbing lit cigarettes into their faces, by giving them electric shocks on the genitals. The senior officer would decide who was to be killed after the interrogation. Most of the leaders or the more educated ones were killed. Their wives would also be interrogated, tortured, and killed."

Indonesia's systematic extermination of East Timor's people rivals the killing fields of Cambodia and the death camps of Nazi Germany. But it can hardly be dismissed as simply the handiwork of a deranged dictator. After all, it was the United States that helped engineer the rise to

Following tradition, every time a close relative has died, this Dani woman has cut off part of a finger.

power of President Suharto in 1968. And in the ensuing years, it was the American fear of communism that drew the United States into ever deeper complicity with this anti-Communist leader, who masterminded one of the most ruthless regimes of the twentieth century.

"I know of the great strides made by Indonesia in nation building under your leadership," said President Reagan, in welcoming Suharto to the United States in 1982. "I am sure that our talks during your state visit will further strengthen the bonds of friendship and mutual respect between our two countries. The United States applauds Indonesia's quest for what you call 'national resilience.'"

It would be wrong to single out Ronald Reagan for criticism, for every U.S. president since Gerald Ford has, by action or inaction, supported Indonesia's war against its indigenous people. The shipment of U.S. arms has continued, and since 1975, the United States has opposed ten United Nations resolutions condemning the illegal invasion of East Timor.

In 1986, Indonesia sent fifteen thousand troops to East Timor and launched "Operation Extinction" to carry out reprisals against innocent civilians following attacks by resistance forces. The Maubere still resisted. In 1988, the Indonesians increased their combat force to twenty-five thousand. By 1990, they had forty thousand troops in East Timor and were proceeding with a transmigration program scheduled to bring in five million Javanese people to settle on the island. Before the 1975 invasion, the East Timorese people had numbered six hundred and fifty thousand. By 1993, at least a third of them had been killed.

For the Maubere to survive, peace must be restored. And for peace to come to East Timor, the human rights of the Maubere people must be secured. Outnumbered, outgunned, and having no prospect of military victory, the Maubere still refuse to give up. "The genocide campaign," says one resistance leader, "has reinforced the determination of the Maubere people to fight the foreign occupation."

Indonesia's annexation of East Timor is remarkably similar to Iraq's attempted takeover of Kuwait in 1990. A 1975 U.N. resolution called "on all states to respect the territorial integrity of East Timor, as well as the inalienable right of its people for self-determination." But this U.N. resolution produced no rescue effort. For nearly twenty years, neither the United States nor any other country has stepped forward to assist the people of East Timor.

❖

It may be that the Maubere, Dani, Moi, and other indigenous peoples of Indonesia will soon be pushed over a threshold of no return. There is no reason to believe that the government will have a sudden change of heart. But as desperate as the situation is, it can still be reversed.

Those of us who live in the industrialized world share a large part of the responsibility for the assault on these people and their lands. And we are the only ones with the power to halt it. We can demand that no more foreign aid be sent to Indonesia until it begins to protect its indigenous peoples. We can insist that the World Bank stop supporting countries that use transmigration and other policies of genocide against indigenous peoples. We can urge adoption of the Declaration of Indigenous Rights developed by the United Nations. We can refuse to buy cabinets, tables, chairs, and other items made from tropical hardwood trees. And we can make it clear to Indonesia that we will not be vacationing in Bali, no matter how beautiful its beaches, how exotic its food, how enticing "the Balinese Cultural Night at the moonlit open-air stage."

A Dani tribesman. Dani boys pierce their noses at the age of fourteen,
and as men will often wear pig tusks during ceremonies.

RECLAIMING AOTEAROA

D o you want to hit a few?"

I glanced up from practicing my tennis serve and saw a man looking at me. He was about thirty and had a mane of black wavy hair down to his shoulders. I had some time to kill, so I answered, "Sure." He introduced himself as Terangi Wharamate, a Maori from New Zealand—in Anchorage, my hometown, he was a long way from home. We played a few sets of tennis that day, a few the next, and before long we'd become good buddies. We shared a love of sports, went kayaking along the Alaska coast, built a few houses, and spent a lot of nights just talking about life. In time, we came to love each other. And this was a new experience for me, really loving another man—not romantically, but like a brother. We shared everything and were always there for each other.

Eventually, Terangi returned to New Zealand—or Aotearoa, as the Maori call their homeland—and a few years passed before I got down there to see him. Within an hour of my landing in Auckland, he had me working with him and his seventy-four-year-old father building a house. That night, Terangi looked troubled and suggested we go for a walk. It was a dark night, brilliant with stars. In a broad meadow a couple of hundred yards out from the house, he stopped and said, "Art, there's something I've got to tell you. You remember when we first met and I told you I went to high school in England?"

"Yeah, Eton right? That famous English school?"

"That's what I told you, but it never happened. I made it up. I guess I just wanted you to accept me, to be my friend."

I told Terangi it didn't matter. We hugged. And that was that. But not quite. As I got to know his family and other Maoris, I began to realize that the little embellishment Terangi had given to his background was symptomatic of the widespread shaming the Maoris had experienced at the hands of New Zealanders of European descent.

"I was never accepted in school," said Terangi, a gifted student and athlete. "I always felt on the outside. Sometimes I wished I was white so I'd have the same rights and privileges the whites had. Art, it felt so good to get away from New Zealand."

A Haka war dance at the opening of the Commonwealth Games, Auckland 1990. In 1993 there were three hundred thousand Maoris in New Zealand, 9 percent of the total population.

Terangi Wharamate. "In my father's generation there was no animosity. What's happening in New Zealand now is a recipe for disaster. Change must come from within."

Terangi escaped, but for most of his generation there was no way out. Some became despondent and found their lives suspended on a string of welfare checks. Others were consumed by rage and ended up in jail. Much like the victims of the Great Death in Alaska, young Maoris had to fight the feeling that something was wrong with them, a suspicion that they had some fatal flaw.

"Like Alaska natives, my ancestors were traumatized by a Great Death," wrote Maynard Gilgin, a Maori psychologist, to Yup'ik leader Harold Napoleon after reading Harold's paper, *Yuuyaraq.* "In the early 1880s, Maori culture was attacked physically, spiritually, and culturally through disease, land confiscation, and the introduction of alcohol. We have journeyed down the road of abuse, using a range of coping mechanisms that included self-blame, alcohol abuse, violence amongst ourselves, depression, denial, and suicide.".

On a day off from work, Terangi, Jo, his English wife, and their two small children traveled with me up to the Bay of Islands, where Terangi had grown up. As we drove past farms with rolling green fields dotted with sheep, cattle, and horses, Terangi said, "Lovely country, isn't it? But this pleasant land is seething under the surface. Now there's a rape, murder, or assault every day. There is a sickness in this society now, and it's malignant."

He shook his head. "You know, New Zealand is headed for disaster. Our timber, our fishing rights—the government has just come in and taken them. A lot of rural Maori have nothing, no way to live, so they've come to hate whites. There are twenty-year-old kids consumed with anger. They are on the dole and they know their kids will be on the dole, and their grandchildren, too. A confrontation is coming and it could bring violence on a grand scale."

I asked him how he and his family fit into all this. After all, he had a white wife.

"It's not an easy question to answer. You know, I get along with anyone, but I understand the hatred and mistrust. On this little island we have two cultures, two completely different ways of viewing life. My culture is based on knowledge. The white culture seems to be based on money and being smart enough to get it any way you can. We respect our elders, but look at what you do to yours. They could be your best teachers, sharing their knowledge and love, but you put them away, out of sight, in old folks' homes."

In Waitangi, Terangi and I walked out over the broad lawns overlooking the Bay of Islands, filled with sailboats and yachts. Right here, two hundred years ago, we might have looked out to see huge Maori war canoes, each manned by a hundred and eighty men. It was at this very spot in February 1840 that the pivotal event in Maori history took place—the signing of the treaty of Waitangi. This was a contract between two nations—the British and the Maori chiefs. But there were two versions of this treaty—thirty people signed the English version; more than five hundred signed the one written in Maori. The latter clearly stated that the Maori retained their *te tino Rangatiratanga*—control over their resources and destiny. But during the past one hundred and fifty years, New Zealanders have found any number of ingenious ways to dispossess the Maoris of their lands.

For example, in 1909 the Native Land Bill was supposed to benefit Maoris. But as the attorney general acknowledged, it helped every

A Maori man with designs of traditional tattooing. "I think people everywhere have gifts and wisdom," says Maori activist Pauline Tangiora. "But today many cultures are lost in the haste of a materialistic world."

European settler to get Maori land. The government established a fund to help Maoris develop their lands, but more money was made available to white settlers to buy Maori lands.

After World War II, the Pakeha, as white New Zealanders are called, returning from combat received generous land grants and farm development loans. "Our people risked their lives, too, and got neither respect nor help in restoring their lives," said Terangi. "After the war, there wasn't an explicit policy of destroying us, but we gradu-

ally lost our lands and our fisheries. We were just fodder in the white man's war, nothing more."

In the 1990s, the situation remains unchanged. On December 10, 1992, I heard Dr. Timothy Reedy tell the U.N. General Assembly in New York that past abuses of the Waitangi Treaty have run Maori unemployment up to 40 percent, four times the national average. And he decried a government proposal to force the sale of Maori fishing rights that had been guaranteed by the treaty. "This bill will trample not only treaty rights, but also aboriginal rights. And it will deny basic human rights to Maori people. Our country's government acts in utter violation of the rights of its indigenous minority."

As I traveled around Aotearoa, one Maori after another described to me how his or her life had been affected by the Pakeha society. I spent a day with Terangi's cousin Nigil, the youngest person ever allowed into the North Auckland group of elders. "Maoris fill the prisons," Nigil told me. "So the question has to be asked: Are Maoris born evil? Or is the system inappropriate for us? I was born of lovely parents. They were both ridiculed and beaten on the hands and the back of the legs for speaking our language."

One night, Terangi and I had dinner with Pauline Tangiora, a Maori activist. She has thirty-six grandchildren, "and every one of them," she told me fiercely, "is going to be proud of being Maori." Pauline said that to her this means "being able to be who you are whenever you feel like it—not being condemned because you might have an odd sock on or your hair is down and blowin' in the wind." She allowed that the Maori may never get all their lands back, but insisted "we recognize that within New Zealand there are two nations of people. If the Pakeha accepted this and acknowledged our right to exist on the land, we'd have the most wonderful country in the world. But fear of losing power is holding them back."

Another day, I visited a high school, where one of Terangi's brothers, Hone, taught Maori studies. A large, somewhat ferocious-looking man, Hone has dedicated his life to teaching children, Maori and Pakeha alike. When I asked him what the future holds for the young Maori, Hone explained that the schools have always presented the Pakeha culture as superior. "Maoris feel inferior. The majority of my Maori students have been traumatized by the education system by the time they reach high school. Every Maori child is a displaced person. They know they are not European. They look Maori. But they don't know who they are. We've already lost a genera-

tion of kids." After a pause he said, "We could be looking at guerrilla warfare. Once the kids see that they are not wanted for who they are, there could be anarchy."

Another Maori teacher said, "I wasn't given a Maori class to teach, but a class of shattered youngsters to care for. I see these girls coming into high school after eight years in the system completely battered and bruised. They have little confidence. Their behavior reflects their inner pain and confusion. And all the school does is yell at them, punish them, expel them."

"Yes, we've been an endangered people," said Hone, "about as endangered as you can get. But we're turning it around." He described the revolution that is taking place, not with armed men, politicians, or lawyers—but with preschool children. With their language and culture rapidly slipping away, a handful of older Maoris formed the first *kohungareo*, a "language nest," in which young Maori children are exposed to the native language and ways of their people. "It's an initiative born out of a people's search for their identity," said Hone. "It's born out of a fear of losing our children."

One afternoon, I watched children, some of them barely old enough to walk, chattering away in Maori as they played games. Later, at lunch at her house, I talked with Ellemain Emery, who directs the *kohungareos* in the Auckland area. She told me that when she first heard about a language nest her mind flashed back to her own childhood. "I knew this was it," she said. "This is what we'd needed all these years. So I got up and told my husband, 'Clear the bottom floor.' 'For what?' he asked. 'Just take that wall out, move it over there.' He said, 'I don't want to do that. It's too expensive.' And I said, 'No, it isn't. We've got to do this for the children, for all of us.'"

Children were everywhere at Ellemain's house. Some of her own brood of nine wandered in and out of the kitchen while we talked, and a dozen or so preschoolers scurried about the lower-floor classrooms. Eventually, these children may be able to continue their bicultural education all the way through high school.

"This may sound strange to you, but relearning our language and culture is the most important health initiative we can take," said Ellemain. "The biggest challenge we face today is regaining our Maori perspective. We need to go back to being people who think in terms of the needs of others. Learn to be kind in the Maori way, be grateful for what you have instead of asking for too much. Notice when your neighbor feels pain, sorrow, sickness.

"Look, we're not rejecting everything that's British. We don't want to go back to the forest and eat nothing but yams and pippies. It can't be done. But we have to try to rebalance things. And unless we do, we will continue to deteriorate to the point of extinction."

I asked Ellemain what she would ask of the Pakeha. "Just be sensitive," she said. "Realize they are living on land that their ancestors stole from the Maori. We are saying to them, 'Don't feel guilty about this situation, just understand it. And now let's work together to make this country bicultural. We can start with the children.'"

Ellemain Emery, Auckland director of kohungareos, or "language nests."
"To stem the loss of our culture and our way of life, we must teach the children
to speak Maori and be proud to be Maori."

ABORIGINES

"WE ARE STILL HERE"

My fascination with the Aborigines of Australia began when I was a child growing up in a small town in Colorado. I can still remember some of the images that called to me from the pages of an old *National Geographic* magazine—a group of naked children playing by a stream, a solitary Aborigine walking across the desert, the eyes of an old man mysterious and calm in his dark face. These people seemed closer to nature than I, free and untroubled. Years later, after moving to Alaska, I came across a sobering account of the Australian Aborigines. Written by an Aboriginal man named J. T. Patton, the article burst my childhood fantasies about a simple, carefree life.

"Our self-respect has been taken away from us, and we have been driven towards extermination," wrote Patton in an early issue of the *Abo Call*, the first Aboriginal newspaper, which he founded in 1938. "We have been called a 'dying race,' but we do not intend to die. We intend to live, and to take our place in the Australian community as citizens with full equality. The white community must be made to realize that we are human beings, the same as themselves. We do not wish to go back to the Stone Age. And we don't want charity from the white people, we want justice. We intend to work steadily for this aim, no matter how many years it may take."

J. T. Patton, I learned, was a founding father of the Aboriginal rights movement. Like Gandhi in India and Martin Luther King, Jr., in the United States, he had been arrested many times for encouraging his people to stand up for their rights. For most of my life, I've lived about as far from Australia as anyone could, but in December 1991 a chance encounter brought Patton's world much closer to me. At a gathering of grass-roots leaders in Paris, someone introduced me to an Aboriginal woman named Pauline Gordon. She was J. T. Patton's daughter.

"I'm just an ordinary person who goes around talking with people," she said. "I pop up here and I pop up there. I'm a member of the Bunjalung tribe on the coast

An Aboriginal boy has caught a large lace-backed goanna lizard, a traditional delicacy.

An Aboriginal elder. "Until the Australian government recognizes the sovereignty of the Aboriginal people, they can talk until they are blue in the face," says Cecil Patton. "We'll keep fighting until we regain our independence."

of New South Wales. That's where I come from. My mother's totem is the possum, my father's was the goanna lizard. My husband's is the dingo. He says I talk too much."

And Pauline *is* quite a talker. When we sat down to visit over lunch, she held forth in her warm voice and lively accent on everything from Aborigine Dreamtime to her own grandchildren. Her brother Cecil, she told me, helps run the Aboriginal Legal Services in Sydney. Her sons, Kenny and Shane, play the digeridoo—a musical instrument made from a hollow tree limb that makes a haunting sound—paint, and are going through their tribe's tradition of initiation into manhood. I began to sense that, in one way or another, Pauline's whole family was carrying on the work begun by J. T. Patton sixty years before. Our lunch lasted seven and a half hours, a record for me. And by the time we said good bye, Pauline

was insisting that I come down to Australia to visit her family.

And so I did. The following March, I flew to Sydney and then caught a flight up the coast to Grafton. On this last leg of my journey, a well-dressed young white woman sat next to me, and before long she asked me where I was going in Australia. To visit a friend in a little place called Baryulgil, I said. "What's it like out there?"

"But . . . nothing's out there," she stammered, unable to comprehend why anyone would come to Australia just to visit an Aboriginal community. "You have to be careful going around those places. I grew up thirty-five miles from Baryulgil and I've never been there once."

"So how do people around here feel about these Aborigines?" I asked.

"Oh, some want to get rid of them," she said. "Some want them to just disappear. And others like me just want to avoid them."

✦

The drive out to Baryulgil took me into some of the most beautiful country I'd ever seen. Here, close to the east coast, the land was many shades of green. There were broad meadows of green and golden grass and gum trees with their leaves shimmering green and silver in the breeze. Dark pines dotted the hills; creeks wandered through the valleys. Now and then a pair of brightly colored parrots would zip by in a hurry to get somewhere. As soon as I got to the little settlement of Baryulgil, Pauline, her husband, Linc, and their sons took me out to a large stream that tumbles over well-worn rocks. The boys, now in their mid-twenties, leapt barefoot from boulder to boulder. When Shane reached a large rock ledge in the middle of the stream, he started playing his digeridoo. Its haunting tones mingled with the sounds of running water. When he moved the hollow end close to a cleft in the rock, the tone changed to a deeper, humming sort of growl that seemed to come out of the earth itself.

An Aboriginal man paints his face with white ochre before dancing.

The rock, I realized, had become an extension of Shane's instrument, of his music, and himself.

"There's an old Aboriginal saying that 'we don't own the land, the land owns us,'" said Pauline. "We think of ourselves as custodians of the land, and the land's not just soil and rock to us. It's the whole of creation—all the land, water, and air, and the life everywhere, people, too. All these things are related and linked together in the Dreamtime. So you see, Aboriginals are part of the land and it is part of them. When we lose our land, we lose a part of ourselves."

❖

Europeans sailed into Sydney Cove on January 26, 1788. The first settlers, many of them convicts exiled from the British Isles, viewed the spacious reaches of Australia as *Terra Nullis*, an empty land. Unlike the volatile Maoris, the Aborigines were gentle and offered little resis-

tance. As a consequence, the British settled Australia without bothering to make any pacts or treaties. As J. T. Patton told it, "From the time of that first settlement in 1788, the Crown has blatantly taken our land without treaty, without purchase, and without compensation of any kind." Two hundred years later, *Terra Nullis* is still a guiding principle in Australia's law. And the dehumanizing acts committed in its name still haunt Aboriginal people.

"They called our land *Terra Nullis* because they wanted to take it from us," said Pauline. "Now, what chance did the old Abo have against all their bloody guns? The settlers just slaughtered our people. We were classified as animals, like kangaroos or dingos. That's what my father fought against all his life. They'd take a mob of black folks and shoot them, or take them down to a creek and drown them, or give them blankets infected with smallpox. In the early days, there were no white women in the country, so to satisfy their lust the settlers raped black women. The black man couldn't do anything about it, he just had to sit there and watch his wife be raped. It was just another way of dragging him down."

In contrast to the rough and rapacious liaisons of the Australian frontier, the Aborigines had strict codes of sexual conduct. They believed that babies are conceived not only from the union of a man and a woman, but out of a dreaming place on the land. Pauline told me, "One day, I asked my mother, 'Mom, where's my dreaming place?' And she took me up in the hills and showed me a waterfall. 'That's your dreaming place,' she told me. 'When you die you'll go back in there. And you'll be there forever. You'll be in that waterfall, watching the seasons come and go like your spiritual ancestors. In that spot, you will be part of the land.' That is why we teach you not to harm or even mark the land. That would be like getting a knife and cutting yourself."

The Aboriginal relationship with the land began with the creation ancestors. They moved over the land, forming mountain ranges, deserts, rivers, trees, and creeks. When all the creating was done, said Pauline, as if she'd just seen it with her own eyes, "those creation beings went back into those trees, logs, and creeks. So the land isn't empty to us, it's alive—alive with our people.

"When white people see black fellows around a campfire, they think, 'Oh, look at those lazy people just sittin' around.' But, hey, that campfire is playing a very important part in Aboriginal life. In the old days, the elders and fully initiated men sat over to one side. Each child had a particular position around that campfire. And when the men came back from hunting, they'd do a dance about what happened that day. All the people in camp would sit back and enjoy themselves. Then someone else would jump up and start dancing or telling a legend.

"They learned that you take only what you need. You didn't kill six kangaroos and hang 'em up to dry. You hunted for food for the day and shared it amongst the tribe. Selfishness was a cardinal sin. Everything had to be shared.

"Now even though we wear clothes, we still do a lot of these tribal things. Like swapping tucker. We might be camping at the riverside in the spring, and we'll say, 'Hey, let's take some meat to the people who live downriver and swap them for pippies and shells and mussels.'"

Many young Aborigines were pulled from tribal life by the government's policy of assimilation, which included the practice of taking small children from their parents and sending them off to boarding schools. "They grabbed us kids, along with thousands of others all around Australia. This was kept from the public, mind you," said Pauline, talking faster as she became more emotional. "I'll never forget the day I went away on the steam train with my sisters. I was only eight, and I asked, 'What's wrong with us, Mom? Why is it everyone is down on Abos? Why's it a sin to be an Aborigine?'"

It was a story I had heard many times in my interviews for this book. From the United States to Indonesia and Africa to here in Australia, the governments in power seemed to tacitly agree that the way to dismantle an indigenous culture was through its children.

Pauline was sent to a girls' home, where she lived until she was eighteen. "I think there are two ways to see it," she said. "I got a good education out of it. But then, what's this white man's education all about? Education for what? To destroy my people? To destroy the land? *Our* education, Aboriginal education, was for survival, for getting along with each other and all the creatures. Theirs was to try to make us be like them.

"I know it's a white man's world now. I know that. I know we can't turn the bloody clock back. But we can still fight to retain our identity, our language, and our pride in who we are. The government cooks up programs to help us now, but they never work. And the reason is, the government broke the cycle. The whites in power broke our cultural cycle. But you can't get them to understand. So we've sort of drifted along. Among ourselves, we call this the last generation."

❖

Sometimes, I went with Linc and the boys up into the rain forest, where the light shimmered through the leaves and vines, and tiny bell birds, too small and wary to be seen, announced our arrival with high ringing calls. Once, wading in a clear cool stream, I came

face to face with a huge eel that rose from the shadows to guard its pool. And one night, Kenny and Shane took me out to a secluded clearing by a river. There, under the stars they shared with me some of the things their people have been doing around campfires for thousands of years. "Australians have no idea that we still do these things," said Shane. In keeping with tradition, what we shared and experienced around that fire and under the immensity of stars remains there with the night.

"You can hardly practice these traditions when you're living in a white man's world," Pauline said later. "They tried to destroy our culture. They

Aboriginal women painting. "Through Aboriginal eyes," says Pauline Gordon, "all the mountains and the whole earth are alive. The landscape tells stories from the dreaming, when the creative times happened."

are still, *still*, trying to assimilate us, to make us disappear into their world."

Then Pauline voiced a sentiment that I'd first heard long ago on the shores of the Bering Sea. "Please try to fathom our great desire to live in a way somewhat different from yours," the Yup'ik elders of Nightmute had said, and I've heard these words echoed by indigenous people everywhere. Why is it so difficult for people from dominant cultures, including my own, simply to accept others as they are? I've heard many native people call the whites' resistance to other ways arrogance, pure and simple. But beneath the arrogance there seems to lie a fear—that if we allow others to be themselves we will somehow be diminished. I asked Pauline if she and her family ever feel bitter.

"That's the funny part about it. Aboriginal people haven't got any hate. We haven't got that emotion. The only thing that I can't forgive is them stealing all those years I could have had with my father. He died right after I got out of the boarding school.

"But I can still remember him saying, 'Okay, kids, come here and have a look. Now, Pauline, see that star up there?' And I'd say, 'Where?' 'Near the moon,' he'd say. 'Now you watch that star. Every night it will get closer and closer and then it will kiss the tip of the moon.' And he told me the legends and the ancestral dreaming stories of that star and how it moves across they sky.

"We may not be bitter, but we know sorrow. Look how this crazy mainstreaming has got our kids drinking and punching needles into their veins. Down in the slummy areas of Sydney they're on drugs and poppin' pills. It makes me real sad. My boys take those kids out to the scrub and teach them to hunt, show them how to dive for turtles. Those young urban blacks are losing touch with their cultural roots. They *sort* of know who they are, but they need more of that Aboriginal spirit in them. We need to feed that Aboriginality."

For perhaps the thousandth time, I thought of the Eskimo youth of the far north drinking and drugging themselves to death. I thought of the frustrated, angry youth of South Africa striking out with violence at one another. I thought of the young blacks of the U.S. inner cities, walking the streets at high risk to their lives.

I thought with emotion of my friend Harold Napoleon and his suffering over the loss of his young son. On a gut level, my travels and these deep, searching conversations were revealing, time and time again, how a government's institutionalized disrespect can become, when internalized, a powerful destructive force.

❖

I visited Pauline's brother Cecil in his office at the Aboriginal Legal Services in Sydney. We spoke about the government's proposal to foster a "reconciliation" intended to resolve the "Aboriginal problem."

"Oh, yeah, sure. They're talkin' reconciliation," he said, in a warm voice similar to Pauline's. Cecil's hair was turning silver, but he looked youthful. He said, "To us *reconciliation* implies that at one stage there was a union between us and the settlers, a friendship or relationship that's broken down. But we've made no deals, no treaties, no agreements. We *want* a treaty, but without the government's recognition of us as a sovereign nation of people there can be no treaty. That's the guts and bone of the matter right there. Without our sovereign rights as human beings, there can be no talk of 'reconciliation.'"

❖

There can, of course, be no reconciliation for those who have disappeared, for the people whose songs and ways of looking at the universe have already vanished. When the Europeans arrived in Australia, two hundred and fifty aboriginal cultures with their own languages lived there.

Today, only a hundred languages are still spoken, and 90 percent of these are close to extinction. Two hundred years of *Terra Nullis* have nearly made Australia's extreme form of racism a self-fulfilling prophesy.

And yet, just before I returned to Alaska, Pauline pulled me aside and said, "Art, I want to tell you what I tell my kids. 'Our culture hasn't disappeared. Hey, we never lost it. It's still here.' The land and the laws are still in existence and rotating. They're alive. You feel it in the bush. Oh, my God! Sometimes, you feel like you want to cry. It's a very powerful spiritual feeling that makes you feel humble.

"Now, every Abo who walks the land pricks the white man's conscience. They did their utmost to wipe us clean off the land, but they did not succeed. We are still here, and for all their trouble to 'educate' and 'assimilate' us, we are still Aborigines."

Aboriginal children.

W hen I began writing this book several years ago, I thought that 1993, the Year of the World's Indigenous Peoples, might become a turning point in the struggle of these groups to survive. But for all the good intentions of the United Nations, its member states have made little more than token gestures toward the rights and needs of indigenous peoples. Far from assuring the cultural survival of these peoples, we are just beginning to understand the extent of the problem.

By some estimates, about two hundred thousand indigenous people a year are being killed. This is many more times the number of U.S. troops killed in Vietnam, casualties that sent a generation of Americans into shock. And the slaughter goes on year after year. Linguists now predict that fewer than half the world's six thousand languages will survive our children's generation. In the coming century, 90 percent of humankind's languages are likely to disappear. Perhaps the most astonishing thing about this unprecedented loss of humanity is that so few people seem to notice. In North America, for example, fifty-one languages have become extinct in just the last thirty years. But who can name even one of them? Who knows who these people were?

When are we going to draw that proverbial line in the sand and say, "Enough is enough"? It is true that we have no easy solutions, no tourniquet that can quickly stem this hemorrhaging of humanity. But, as indigenous leaders have been urging, certain important steps could make a real difference. The United Nations could adopt a strong Declaration of Indigenous Rights. Multinational corporations could routinely assess the effects of their activities on indigenous peoples. The developed countries of Europe, North America, and Asia could stop sending aid to countries that blatantly violate the human rights of native peoples. Churches could begin respecting indigenous beliefs, songs, and dances. The World Bank and other lending agencies could reconsider the progress-fixated world view that has dictated their decisions and undermined so many indigenous cultures. And wherever we live we could demand that our governments protect native lands and ways of life, and the people's right to worship.

I'm afraid, however, that even the best laws, treaties, covenants, policies, and initiatives will be of limited value unless all people come to respect and value "the Other." Such an affirmation of humanity, *all* humanity, can only begin close to home—with the world's children, its schools, and its communities. Only from expressions of mutual respect on a small, local scale will it be possible to foster a broadened sense of responsibility.

In the global activities of nation-states and multinational corporations, lines of responsibility become obscure and hard to trace. Caught up with the busyness of our daily lives, we tend not to notice what is happening on the other side of the earth. It is not that we are callous or mean-spirited, but that living in a global community requires a kind of understanding that we have yet to develop.

But is "the Other," on the other side of the fence or the other side of the world, really such a mystery? Don't most of us work toward the same life goals—to provide food, shelter, and clothing for our families, to raise our children in peace, and to live in a clean and healthy environment? Native or nonnative, we all share hopes and dreams for a sense of safety and the opportunity to live life as we understand it. I remember Pauline Tangiora of Aetearoa saying that "Europeans have never liked to feel that they are a part of us. But they are also people of the land. It's time to lay down the barriers and say 'join in.' If you can share my world as a Maori, share my language, the thought patterns of my people, then we're both enriched. Because I've already had to share yours."

In the end, then, the answer to this daunting challenge to the world's cultural diversity is, in principle, dismayingly simple. We need to acknowledge that diversity is the great wellspring of humanity's strength, and then work as partners—all of us—to preserve it. I recall an Aboriginal woman telling some concerned Australians, "If you've come here to save us, then go on home. But if you've come to struggle with us on our common problems, then let's get to work."

If readers of this book want to become involved in the struggles of indigenous peoples, I suggest contacting one or more of the following organizations. Most of them publish well-researched reports, newsletters, and action alerts. All of these organizations do excellent work and welcome participation and support of their ongoing efforts on behalf of endangered peoples.
A.D.

Amnesty International
322 8th Avenue
New York, New York 10001
Phone: (212) 291-9233
Amnesty International calls on governments to honor treaties and international conventions that protect human rights.

Assembly of First Nations
Territory of Akwesasne
Hamiltons Island, Summerstown
Ontario, Canada
Phone: (613) 931-1012
Fax: (613) 931-2438
As the national representative of indigenous nations in Canada, the Assembly of First Nations advocates for a wide range of social, economic, land, and human rights reform.

Association on American Indian Affairs
245 Fifth Avenue, Suite 1801
New York, New York 10016
Phone: (212) 689-8720
Fax: (212) 685-4692
This organization heads the Religious Freedom Coalition, which is seeking to amend the American Indian Religious Freedom Act. It also assists tribes in the protection of sacred sites.

Cordillera Peoples Alliance
Lock Box 596 GARCOM-Baguio
P.O. Box 7691 DAPO 1300
Pasay City, Philippines
The Cordillera Peoples Alliance is an active grass roots organization working for the rights and well-being of the Igorot people of the Philippine Cordillera. The Alliance welcomes inquiries about and support for the struggle of these indigenous peoples.

Cultural Survival, Inc.
215 First Street
Cambridge, Massachusetts 02142
Phone: (617) 495-2562
Cultural Survival is an international advocate for the human rights of endangered peoples. Founded in 1972, it supports a wide range of projects and publishes *Cultural Survival Quarterly.*

Endangered Peoples Project
Box 1516 Station A
Vancouver, British Columbia V6C 2P7
Canada
The Endangered Peoples Project was founded by a small group of environmental and indigenous rights activists, who have been very effective in spearheading campaigns in such diverse regions as Sarawak, West Papua New Guinea, Brazil, Guatemala, and Zaire.

Grand Council of the Crees
24 Bayswater Avenue
Ottawa, Ontario K1Y 2E4
Canada
Phone: (613) 761-1655
Fax: (613) 761-1388
The Grand Council is the tribal organization of the Crees, which is mounting resistance to the expansion of the James Bay hydroelectric project.

Gwich'in Steering Committee
Box 202768
Anchorage, Alaska 99503
Phone: (907) 258-6814
The Gwich'in Steering Committee is the tribal organization fighting to protect the Porcupine caribou herd and the traditional ways of the Gwich'in people in Alaska and Canada. The Gwich'in welcome support in their battle to protect the caribou calving grounds.

Human Rights Committee for Non-Burman Nationalities
P.O. Box 118
Chiang Mai 50000
Thailand
This organization, working in exile, fights for the human rights of Burma's indigenous minorities.

Indian Council of Indigenous and Tribal Peoples
28 Mahadev Road
New Delhi 110001
India
This nongovernmental organization works with a wide range of tribal people throughout the subcontinent of India, providing both information and direct assistance.

Indigenous Survival International
298 Elgin Street, Suite 105
Ottawa, Ontario K2P 1M3
Canada
Phone: (613) 230-3616
Fax: (613) 230-3595
This organization works with indigenous peoples from
Alaska, Canada, and Greenland to protect the traditional
cultures of the far north.

International Indian Treaty Council
1259 Folsom
San Francisco, California 94103
Phone: (415) 512-1501
This council represents a network of indigenous peoples
trying to secure their rights through treaties, many of
which have been ignored for generations.

International Working Group for Indigenous Affairs
Fiolstraede 10
DK-1171 Copenhagen K
Denmark
Phone: 45-33-124-724
Fax: 45-33-147-749
IWGIA exposes the oppression of indigenous peoples
through wide-ranging research and the publication of
documents, newsletters, and yearbooks, which provide
excellent up-to-date information and analysis of
indigenous issues throughout the world.

OPM (Free Papua Movement)
PIO Box 11582
The Hague
Netherlands
OPM works in exile for the liberation and rights of
more than three hundred tribal peoples in West Papua
New Guinea.

Rainforest Action Network
450 Sansome Street
San Francisco, California 94111
Phone: (415) 398-4404
Fax: (415) 398-2732
RAN works with organizations in more than sixty countries
to preserve rain forests and support the struggles of
indigenous peoples within the forests. It publishes alerts,
resource packets, and a quarterly newsletter.

Sarawak Peoples Campaign
Box 344
Station A
Vancouver, British Columbia V6C 2M7
Canada
Phone: (604) 669-5444
Fax: (604) 687-5575
This international advocacy group works for protection
of enough of the Sarawak rain forest to ensure the survival
of the Penan and twenty-five other indigenous peoples.

Survival International
310 Edgeware Road
London W2 IDY
United Kingdom
Phone: 44-71-723-5535
Fax: 44-71-723-4059
Survival International works for tribal peoples by lobbying
governments and conducting on-site protests and demon-
strations. The group publishes reports, newsletters, and
action bulletins through offices in the United Kingdom,
Italy, France, and Spain.

Tibetan Rights Campaign
Box 31966
Seattle, Washington 98103
Phone: (206) 547-1015
The Washington-based Tibetan Rights Campaign issues
periodic newsletters and sponsors a variety of projects
through which volunteers can work for the liberation
of Tibet and the rights of the Tibetan people.

Vicente Menchú Foundation
Box 5274
Berkeley, California 94705
Phone: (510) 548-6495
Founded by Nobel Laureate Rigoberta Menchú Tum, the
Vicente Menchú Foundation seeks peaceful solutions to
armed conflict and promotes human rights. The foundation
seeks contributions to an endowment dedicated to promot-
ing cultural and ethnic identity, human rights, land reform,
and environmental protection.

World Council of Indigenous Peoples
555 King Edward
Ottawa, Ontario K1N 6N5
Canada
Phone: (613) 230-9030
The WCIP was formed in 1975 to help ensure the social,
cultural, and political development of indigenous peoples.
The council conducts research on alternative models of
development and the impact of national and international
projects on indigenous peoples.

ACKNOWLEDGMENTS

For their thoughtful advice, guidance, and encouragement,
I want to thank Julian Burger, Jens Dahl, Minnie Degawan, Joe Friday, Elias Frenier,
Pauline Gordon, Linda Gunnarson, Sarah James, Viktor Kaisiepo, Patricia Locke, Harold Napoleon,
John Pingayak, Jorge Terena, Mutang Urud, Maria Vasquez, and Terangi Wharamate.

This book could not have been completed without a tremendous team effort
by some very creative and dedicated people. One couldn't have a more supportive publisher than
Jon Beckmann of Sierra Club Books. Editors Suzanne Lipsett, Danny Moses, and David Spinner worked
nights and weekends to help meet deadlines, as did research and production assistants Daniella Gayle and
Daphne Hougard and typesetter Steve Wozenski. Imaginative designer Charles Fuhrman was a joy to work
with. And the photographers! Not only did Art Wolfe and John Isaac donate the use of their photographs,
but the other photographers greatly reduced their rates to contribute to *Endangered Peoples*.

Many others have helped make this book possible.
In particular, I want to acknowledge the contributions of Teresa Aparicio, Maureen Bisilliat,
Simon Brascoupé, Brad Bunnin, Jason Clay, Cabot Christianson, Bernard Comrie, Cathy Conti, Ben Davis,
Wade Davis, Jim Ennis, Mark Faeo, Candice Fuhrman, Dieter Hagenbach, Thom Henley, Holly Henning,
Shane Kennedy, Lindsay Knight, Michael Krause, Roxanne Kremer, Diana Landau, Heidi Larson,
Rachel Lund, Finn Lynge, Ian MacKenzie, Donna Manders, Jerry Mander, Pat Meyer, Betty Mindlin,
Charles Murphy, Bill Namagoose, Herb and Sandy Newburger, Shiro Nishimae, Jim Parrish, Cecil Patten,
Bill Perry, Chris Peters, Dalee Sambo, Karen Serieka, Tom Sexton, Richard Siddle, Tammie Smith,
Beth Stienhorn, Nigil Tairua, Pauline Tangiora, Jim and Jan Thurston, Don Williams,
Samantha Delay Wilson, and Yuko Yoneda.

Finally, a very special thanks to Anna Phillip,
a lovely Yup'ik activist who entered my life while I was working on this book.

PHOTO CREDITS

Art Wolfe: Preface ii–iii, v, viii, Ishi 11, Gwitch'in 24, 27, 28, Andes 62, 64, 68, 69
Amazonia 70, 73, 74, 79, Africa 80–81, Malagasy 96, 98, 99, 101, 103, 104–105
Tibet 116, 117, 118, 119, 121, 123, Ainu 124, 127, 130
Sarawak 132, 137, 139, Pacific Islands 154, 158, 161
Indonesia 170, 173, 174, 177, 179, Maori 183, 185, Aborigines 186, 188, 191
John Isaac: Andes 67, Tuareg 82, 85, 86, 87, Maasai 88, 91, 92, Tibet 114
Southeast Asia 140, 142, 143, 144, 145, 146, 149, 151, Igorot 162
Art Davidson: American Indians 42, Amazonia 76, Sarawak 134
Lionel Delevigne: Ishi 9, 13, Cree 35, 39
Paul Dix: Central America 56
Mark Downey: Preface x, Central America 61, Igorot 165
Robert C. Gildart: Gwich'in 29, 31
Bob Hallinen/*Anchorage Daily News*: Yup'ik 18, 23
Erik Hill/*Anchorage Daily News*: Yup'ik 17, 20
Daphne Hougard: Pacific Islands 153–154
Ivan Hunter/Santa Barbara Museum of Natural History: Ishi 13
Cindy Karp/Black Star: Central America 52
Paul Liebhardt: Central America 55
Robert Madden/National Geographic Society: Amazonia 75, 77
Geoff Mason/Keylight: Maori 180
David Moore/Black Star: Aborigines 189, 193
National Geographic Society: Latin America 50–51
Lito C. Ocampo: Igorot 169
Photo Researchers: Ainu 128
Myron Rosenberg: Yup'ik 14, 19, Russia 106, 110, 113
Kyle Rothenberg: Pacific Islands 157
Paul Souders/*Anchorage Daily News*: Russia 109
Don B. Stevenson: American Indians 49
Mario Tapla/Contact Press Images: Central America 59
R. Dixon, courtesy Department of Library Services, American Museum of Natural History: Ishi 6
Fred Ward/Black Star: Cree 32
Ted Wood: North America 4–5, American Indians 40, 45, Maasai 95